TEACHING FOR LOVE AND JUSTICE

Teaching for Love and Justice

Learning About Race and Racism
Alongside Young Children

Kirsten Cole

www.redleafpress.org
800-423-8309

Published by Redleaf Press
10 Yorkton Court
St. Paul, MN 55117
www.redleafpress.org
© 2026 by Kirsten Cole

All rights reserved. Unless otherwise noted on a specific page, no portion of this publication may be reproduced or transmitted in any form or by any means, electronic or mechanical, including photocopying, recording, or capturing on any information storage and retrieval system, without permission in writing from the publisher, except by a reviewer, who may quote brief passages in a critical article or review to be printed in a magazine or newspaper, or electronically transmitted on radio, television, or the internet.

First edition 2025
Cover design by Michelle Lee Lagerroos
Cover art by Sonia and Tatum
Interior design by Wendy Holdman
Typeset in Karmina

Works by Charles Olson published during his lifetime are copyright the Estate of Charles Olson; previously unpublished works are copyright the University of Connecticut. Used with permission.

Printed in the United States of America

33 32 31 30 29 28 27 26   1 2 3 4 5 6 7 8

Cataloging-in-Publication Data is on file with the Library of Congress

Printed on acid-free paper

In memory of Patricia Carini, Doris Owen, and Charles Ragland.

In honor of my students—past, present, and future.

Contents

Foreword by Samantha R. Diaz
ix

Acknowledgments
xi

Introduction
xiii

CHAPTER 1
Teaching About Race and Racism with Young Children:
Who, What, When, Where, and Why?
1

CHAPTER 2
How We Teach About Race
21

CHAPTER 3
How We Teach About Racism
39

CHAPTER 4
How We Create Anti-Racist Classrooms
57

CHAPTER 5
How We Talk with Families About Race and Racism
93

CHAPTER 6
How We Prepare Educators to Teach About Race and Racism
119

CHAPTER 7
How We Change the World
147

References
151

Index
157

FOREWORD

Teaching for Love and Justice: A Classroom and a Movement

It is an honor to write the foreword for *Teaching for Love and Justice*. Every day I step into my classroom as a teacher, a mother of three boys of color, and as an Afro Latina woman who believes deeply in the capacity of children to see the world clearly and to act with courage and compassion. I know the urgency of raising and educating children in a world marked by racial injustice, and I have seen firsthand how intentional teaching can cultivate empathy, justice, and pride in young learners.

Kirsten Cole's work in my second- and third-grade classroom shows how educators can create spaces that are bilingual, inclusive, and anti-racist. Her writing highlights how teachers can design curriculum and learning experiences that encourage children to explore race, identity, and justice, while also honoring their curiosity, creativity, and voices. She shows how children are not passive learners but active participants capable of grappling with difficult truths and imagining new possibilities.

Children engaged in anti-racist teaching do not experience shame; instead, they leave affirmed, curious, and empowered. They ask questions about race, explore identities, and express themselves through art, writing, and collaboration. The learning becomes both rigorous and deeply human, fostering pride in self and responsibility to community.

Kirsten captures the joy and power of this work. Her careful documentation illustrates how storytelling, literature, and lived experiences serve as powerful tools for awakening children's sense of justice. Teachers, guided by these examples, can design classrooms where children not only learn about history and civil rights but also see themselves as capable of contributing to a more equitable and just world. We can reflect on our own continuous, documented practices and elevate how we guide children toward understanding and acting for justice.

Kirsten's vision brings together research and real classroom practice to provide educators with a guide for fostering justice, equity, and love. By sharing the strategies, reflections, and voices of teachers and children, she offers a resource that can inspire classrooms everywhere to center justice, amplify children's agency, and cultivate communities where every child's identity is valued and affirmed. This book is a testament to the power of documenting and sharing teaching that is grounded in care, reflection, and a commitment to a more just world, and for that, I am deeply grateful.

—Samantha R. Diaz, MS Ed, Dual-Language Special Education Teacher, Doctoral Student at Teachers College, Columbia University

Acknowledgments

This book would not have been possible without the encouragement and wisdom of many. First and foremost, I extend my heartfelt thanks to the educators who generously shared their time, their stories, and their vulnerable self-reflection on the important work that they do. Every time I felt like giving up on the enormous task of writing a book, I remembered that I owed it to the amazing educators I had interviewed to share their wisdom.

It was so important to me to find a good home for this book. Great thanks to Melissa York, Jennifer Anderson, Doug Schmitz, and everyone at Redleaf Press for helping me bring this work into the world. Finding the right publisher allowed me to explore complex ideas with nuance, in my own voice, and to speak directly to my beloved audience of early childhood educators.

I am who I am as a teacher and a writer because I am a member of loving and supportive communities, including my friends and colleagues at the Borough of Manhattan Community College, the Institutes on Descriptive Inquiry, and Brooklyn Quaker Meeting. A few people in my world deserve special mention, because they listened with patience and care as I worked through my ideas (as well as through my imposter syndrome and writer's block!). Much love and gratitude for Dohra Ahmad, Louisa Cruz-Acosta, Samantha Diaz, Krystal Dillard, Ivana Espinet, Jolene Festa, Jessie Fleischer-Black, Brenda Frias, Jen Gilken, Shawn Grant, Charlotte Hunter, Holly Lash, Kirsten Menger-Anderson, Soniya Munshi, Taeko Onishi, Angela Polite, Regan Pritzker, Bonnie Silver, Gail Shust, Angela Taormino, Diandra Verwayne, and Sarah Way.

I was guided from childhood through adulthood with love and integrity by my family, especially my parents Tom and Connie Cole and Carol Owen and Michael Posner. I also thank my siblings Ben, Dinah, Emily, Lauren, and Lindsay, and their beautiful families.

Finally, I don't have words to express how lucky I feel to be a part of Team Frackcole. David, you have been my loving, patient partner and best friend through it all. Max and Zeke, you showed me how to learn alongside young children, and I am so proud to witness the young adults you are becoming.

Introduction

These Days
by Charles Olson

whatever you have to say, leave
the roots on, let them
dangle

And the dirt

                    Just to make clear
                    where they came from

In the early 2000s I was a new teacher. I had worked with children for many years before then in a variety of part-time positions, but my first full-time job was as a teaching artist at a small after-school program housed within the School of Education at a local university. The university had received a federal grant to offer child care to the children of low-income college students. Because of the racial wealth gap in the United States, most of the low-income college student–parents at our program were Black and Latine. I am a White teacher.

    Our program was small, so it essentially functioned as a multi-age classroom. Building relationships was central and we held community meetings every day. We sat in a circle and did a check-in, we read and discussed books, and we worked together to resolve conflicts when they arose. Our curriculum was arts and literacy based, and we explored media and read books that represented a variety of cultures and identities. Unlike most after-school programs, we offered an extended day until 8:45 p.m. to accommodate the schedules of our student–parents who were taking courses in the evening. Additionally, many of the children were with us for several years, for the duration of the time it took for their parents to complete their degrees. We wove, sculpted, and painted together. We wrote poems and plays and shared stories. We ate dinner together. We felt like a family.

I was originally hired as a teaching artist, but when the first director moved upstate, I was hired to replace her. Soon after, I returned from a rare sick day to learn that in my absence an incident had occurred. Six-year-old Brittany (pseudonym), a light-skinned Latina girl, had used the N-word when speaking to seven-year-old Charles (pseudonym), a Black boy. Needless to say, Charles's mother was extremely upset and demanded to know how we would address the issue. When my colleagues told me what had happened, my first reaction was to freeze in fear. How could I, as a White woman, possibly come up with an adequate response to an incident of racism?

According to the most recent data on teacher demographics from the US Department of Education's National Center for Education Statistics (2023a, 2023b), approximately 80 percent of teachers in the United States are White like me. I spent the first several decades of my life striving to be a "good" White person, socialized to believe that I should not consider race, my own or others, in my interactions with other people. My whiteness protected me from understanding the impact that my racial identity has on me and the world. As a child I quickly learned that when it came to race the best thing to do was not to notice it, not to talk about it, not to linger on differences. I believed that racism was something that "bad" White people did by being mean to people of color. I also believed that racist White people were distant from me in time and space, imagining them as figures of the pre–Civil War South or as members of the Ku Klux Klan. Well into my thirties I felt uncomfortable using the phrase "white supremacy" to describe the present. It felt like an extreme and ugly term to use. It wasn't until my forties that I finally began to reckon deeply with the ways that racism and white supremacy are central to the foundation of many of our institutions in the United States. Through listening to and learning from educators, thinkers, colleagues, and friends who hold a variety of racial identities, I came to understand that individual acts of racism are the tip of the iceberg buoyed by a system of structures created to uphold whiteness and marginalize and oppress anyone who is not identified as White. I did not learn these truths in my K-12 education. It took me many years to begin to seek out this education. I know that I will forever be playing catch-up as I learn about race and racism, but I also know that I must continue to learn and grow if I want to be successful as a teacher and to act with integrity as a human being.

All those years ago, when Brittany called Charles a racist word, I did not know what to do. But I knew that we needed to respond. I knew that as a White teacher, my understanding of race and racism would always be incomplete, so I began by talking with my colleagues about what had happened. We discussed all the possible meanings and intention of Brittany's use of the N-word and talked about the impact the incident had on Charles and the other children. Esi, one of our work-study students who had migrated to New York from Ghana to attend college, asked us to explain to her the history of the N-word and the use of it in the United States. Candy, a staff member who identified as Afro-Caribbean, told us that she and her friends used the N-word affectionately when speaking with each other as a way to neutralize the negative power the word has held historically. All of us shared the associations we have with the word, most of which were negative. We debated addressing the issue only with Brittany and Charles, but eventually decided that we needed to have a discussion with the whole community of children and teachers.

That afternoon we sat together in a circle. I explained that someone in our community had recently used a word with a very powerful meaning and we needed to discuss what had happened. I explained that I was going to write the word on the board and quickly erase it. (All the children in our program knew how to read.) I told the community that I, as a White person, choose never to use this word because it has been used by White people to make Black people feel afraid and is sometimes used by White people while they are hurting Black people's bodies. Every child and adult in the circle shared our understanding of the word, and many shared stories of their experiences of racism. We came to a consensus that, because the N-word is often used to hurt people, we would not use it in our community. The conversation took some time, but the children, who could often get wiggly during a long meeting, sat with rapt attention, listening closely as each person spoke. I already had spoken directly with Brittany and her mother about the incident, and no one called her out while we were sitting in the circle. I watched while she listened intently as other children and adults shared the pain associated with the word. That evening I sent a note home with the families to let them know about the conversation and emphasize that I welcomed their thoughts, questions, and feedback.

Brittany, Charles, and all of the other children who were present that day are now in their mid- to late twenties. I still wonder what that conversation meant to them. There are so many other ways we could have responded to that incident. What we did was good, but definitely not perfect. On that day, I felt we had done a good enough job creating a brave space for ourselves and our students to process some hard truths. On other days, I have been crushingly aware of my missteps in responding to race and racism. Years later, I attended a session at a teaching institute where we shared how we were talking with the children in our lives about the increased visibility of police violence against unarmed Black people. As I spoke of how I talked to my young White sons, I was overcome by emotion and began to sob uncontrollably. A young Afro-Latina teacher next to me put her hand on my shoulder as I cried and tried to pull myself together. I knew from the stories she had shared during other sessions that her experiences of racism were much more painful and much more direct than anything I had ever experienced. I give myself some grace for feeling what I felt, but I still wish I had not taken up so much space and energy in that moment. I wish I had not been that White person who needed to be comforted by a person of color as I processed my emotional response to the horrors of racism. I continue to be a work in progress.

Today I work as a teacher educator, teaching and learning alongside my brilliant and beautiful students who are becoming early childhood teachers. Writing this book is a step in my journey to better understand how we can do the essential work of supporting young children's development of a healthy racial identity. In my work as a professor, I learn with my students about child development. We learn methods for designing curriculum. We learn how to build partnerships with families. Through it all, we learn more about race, culture, and identity—our own, our students', and their families'. We do this because, as Candice, one of the thoughtful early childhood educators I interviewed for this book, shared, "Before you can make a kid comfortable enough to read to you or to make mistakes with you, you have to make them feel like a person that you respect. You have to make them feel like they matter." I have written this book in the hope that you and I can learn together from teachers who are doing this essential work with young children. The work is never perfect. It is often messy. But I hope you will agree that this commitment is absolutely central to the work of raising the next generation.

CHAPTER 1

Teaching About Race and Racism with Young Children: Who, What, When, Where, and Why?

You need to be comfortable in your own skin color and to accept other skin colors. Because we need to live together. It's one world, for now. We're not sending anyone to Mars.

—Luísa, interview transcript

Before you can make a kid comfortable enough to read to you or make mistakes with you, you have to make them feel like a person that you respect. You have to make them feel like they matter. So we have a lot of work to do.

—Candice, interview transcript

Who?

I was twenty-one years old when I got my nose pierced. Little did I know that making this somewhat impulsive decision would result in my spending years answering young children's questions about the choice. "What's that thing?" They point with tiny fingers touching the edge of my nostril. "Why did you do that?" As anyone who has spent time with young children knows, their natural curiosity leads them to notice and wonder aloud about the ways that we are different and the ways that we are the same. As children sit beside us and in our laps they stroke the hair on our heads and arms, taking note of differences in color and texture. They peer unblinkingly at our eyes, our noses, our ears. They ask about our tattoos. They wonder aloud if the man at the grocery store has a baby in his belly like their aunt. They are not being rude. They are simply approaching the world with scientific curiosity, seeking to make sense of what's around them. As adults, most of us have spent decades having our ability to express curiosity about difference socialized out of us. Especially for those of us who identify as White, we learn through spoken and unspoken messages that it is taboo to openly observe differences related to race. As a result, we feel uncomfortable and unprepared when responding to children's questions and observations. Children rely on us to help them find answers that will expand their understanding of the world. We let them down when we are not ready to join them in their inquiry.

Discoveries in the science of genetics have confirmed that regardless of the color of our skin or the boxes we check on the census, we are all remarkably similar. In a 2020 *New York Times* article by Natalie Angier, "Do Races Differ? Not Really, Genes Show," Dr. Harold P. Freeman is quoted explaining, "If you ask what percentage of your genes is reflected in your external appearance, the basis by which we talk about race, the answer seems to be in the range of .01 percent." Essentially, when it comes to genetic makeup, all human beings are 99.99 percent alike. Nonetheless, we assign a great deal of importance to that .01 percent of difference. There is excellent scholarship available on the history of how the idea of race and whiteness were invented, how the definitions of racial categories have evolved, and the consequence all of this has had on our lives (see for example Alexander 2011; Kendi 2019; Lee 2005; McGhee 2021; Menakem 2017; Oluo 2018; Sue 2003). The focus of this book is on the consequence of these ideas on how young children grow and learn.

As someone whose career is dedicated to preparing the next generation of early childhood educators, I am continually seeking to learn how early childhood teachers can work to support the healthy racial identity development of young children. On my journey to understand this better, I interviewed twenty-seven early childhood educators. They describe their racial and ethnic identities in a variety of ways: Guyanese, White Italian American, Afro-Latina, Korean American, and more. They work in both public and privately funded settings with children from birth through eight years old. All teach in New York City, where the Department of Education administers the largest school system in the United States. Despite this geographic limitation, it is my hope that readers outside of New York will find points of connection to issues they see in their classrooms and local communities.

As mentioned above, 80 percent of the teaching workforce in the United States consists of White people like me. In many parts of this country, this is not representative of the racial demographics of the children attending our schools. According to the National Center for Education Statistics (2024), as of the fall of 2022, the racial identities of school-aged children in public schools in the United States were 44 percent White, 29 percent Hispanic, 15 percent Black, 5 percent Asian, and 1 percent American Indian/Alaska Native. Five percent of children were identified as biracial or multiracial. Clearly, we must prioritize developing a teaching workforce that is more reflective of the children served. The United States is home to a diverse, multiracial population, though often we still live in segregated communities. Children of all races and ethnicities deserve to see teachers of all races and ethnicities represented. In early childhood education, a field that has historically been undervalued and undercompensated, we do often find more educators of color working in classrooms (NAEYC 2019; Paschall et al. 2023). However, in my work in schools I have observed anecdotally that educators of color are more likely to serve in assistant teacher roles. Lead teachers, who have the responsibility for designing and implementing curriculum, are more often White.

Throughout this book I will primarily be using the term *people of the global majority* in place of the more commonly known *people of color*. *People of color* is inaccurate because it suggests that people who are identified as White do not have a color or race. Whiteness is so often considered the default, the standard, the experience, and the perspective that is "normal" that it does not need to be named. In contrast, people who are not identified as White are understood as different, as nonstandard, as people of color. *People of color* is also a flawed term because it is often used to overgeneralize and homogenize the experiences of people from varied and plural diasporas. The term *people of the global majority* is a more accurate way to refer to people from Asia and the Pacific, from Africa, and from the Americas whose ancestry is not European. It reminds us that whiteness, while hegemonic, is not in fact the majority experience.

Research has demonstrated that students of all races benefit by having educators of color (Cherng and Halpin 2016). People of the global majority living in the United States tend to have lived experiences with race and racism. As educators, they may bring a more informed and nuanced approach to the important task of supporting young children's healthy racial identity development because they are more likely than White people to have experienced firsthand what it means to be excluded, marginalized, or oppressed because of their identity. Educators who are people of the global majority may also have experienced environments and relationships that nurtured their own healthy racial identity development, and consider teaching about the complex topics of race and racism an essential aspect of their work. Most of the teachers I interviewed have engaged in the self-reflective work necessary to understand their own racial identity and to remove the blinders of *color-evasiveness* (Jones 2025) that many of us have been socialized to absorb. Nonetheless, they may not always feel prepared to address issues of race with young children.

In light of this reality, we need to commit to doing two things. First, we need to work intentionally to create an early childhood workforce that is reflective of the racial and ethnic diversity of the children and families that schools serve. Second, we need to provide ongoing training for *all* teachers to strengthen their capacity to teach and learn with young children about race and racism. Supporting young children's healthy identity development is essential to our work in early childhood. All children need opportunities to feel affirmed in their identities and to value and uplift the identities of others. This is central to our work in early childhood, but as many of us did not experience a racially aware approach to education when we were young children, we need ongoing support to develop our capacity to offer it to the next generation. In the chapters to come, we will learn how the educators I interviewed have worked intentionally and thoughtfully to teach and learn about race and racism alongside the children in their care. We will learn of promising practices as well as pitfalls in doing this work, including challenges that may arise when talking about race and racism with families. Finally, we will consider how to support teachers to do this work well.

> What is *color-evasiveness*? In the Fostering Healthy Identity Framework offered by the nonprofit organization Defending the Early Years, this stance is defined as "Believing that it is best to ignore race and treat everyone equally" (Jones 2025). The term is used to replace the ableist language in "racial colorblindness."

What?

There are many wonderful things about our world, many sources of joy and connection. But the world we live in is not yet a truly just and loving place. Violence has been done to the bodies, hearts, and minds of people of the global majority because of a system that falsely asserts the superiority of people who are called White. To move forward toward making the world a more just and loving place, we must work together toward dismantling this unjust and unloving system. No one is born racist. But we are all born into a racist society, and we become socialized to absorb racist ideas starting at an early age. We can create a more just and loving world in the future if we support our children in resisting the racist messages that are all around us. Dr. Beverly Daniel Tatum, scholar and author of the seminal 1997 book *Why Are All the Black Kids Sitting Together in the Cafeteria? And Other Conversations About Race* offers a metaphor for understanding the impact of racism on our lives. She explains that although people living in places with high levels of air pollution would surely prefer not to breathe in smog, it is all around them. Racism, she writes, is like smog. Whether we would like to or not, we breathe it in, absorbing it in our bodies, hearts, and minds. People who live in highly polluted areas have options to reduce their intake of smog. In the short term, they can filter the air in their homes. In the long term, they can decrease the use of instruments of pollution that cause smog. This work is both individual and collective. Similarly, we can work individually to reduce our individual intake of racist beliefs while also working collectively to move away from policies and practices that enact racism.

As adults, we have breathed in the smog of racism for decades. What if we could raise our children in a way that prevents them from absorbing these messages? What if we could join with them in setting aside the instruments of racism? We have extensive documentation of the ways racism harms the bodies, hearts, and minds of people of the global majority. Living in a racist world that privileges people who are called White also harms the moral development of White children. Racism prevents all of us from working together to build a more just and loving world. In writing this book, I wanted to document the ways that early childhood education can contribute to raising children capable of resisting racism, children who can work with us to reduce the impact of racism on our systems, structures, policies, and practices. But before we address racism with young children, we must begin by affirming the healthy racial identity development of every child, as every child deserves to feel fully seen, whole, and affirmed in our classrooms and communities. Therefore, we must begin by talking about race.

Race is a social construct, but it holds great power over how we live. Resmaa Menakem is a wise and spiritually grounded therapist whose 2017 book *My Grandmother's Hands: Racialized Trauma and the Pathway to Mending Our Hearts and Bodies* offers a powerful approach to healing the trauma we all experience from living in a racist world. Menakem reminds us, "For all its fraudulence . . . race is a myth with teeth and claws that continues to tear bodies apart. Institutions, structures, beliefs, and narratives have been created around it. Until we recognize it for the collective delusion it is, it might as well be real" (2017, 68). As we have learned through the research on genetics mentioned above, human beings are 99.99 percent alike in our genetic makeup. There is no fixed formula for what makes a Black person, an Asian person, a White person, a Latine person. In fact, the use of these categories to describe us is a relatively recent development in human history. The meaning of these labels has never been fixed.

The idea of race was invented by human beings to sort, categorize, and assign value and power to some people while diminishing the value of others. The construction of the category of whiteness has been particularly harmful. White colonizers in the United States earned their wealth through killing and stealing land from Indigenous people and by the violent and immoral practice of enslaving people from Africa. These practices were justified by the false assertion of white supremacy. Powerful Whites also relied on the labor of poor Whites. They grew wealthy on the backs of workers of many races who performed under- and uncompensated labor. Whites who exploited others for their own gain saw that if the White and non-White workers came together there was a risk that they might lose power. Thus, the category of whiteness and the toxic myth of the supremacy of White bodies was used as a way to divide a multiracial working class (Kendi 2019; Menakem 2017; McGhee 2021; Oluo 2018).

Racial categories evolve and mutate over time. Immigrants to the United States from Ireland, Italy, and Eastern Europe were not initially granted the status of whiteness. We continue to wrestle with the hypocrisy of celebrating our heritage as a refuge for European immigrants while simultaneously upholding racist, xenophobic laws targeting immigrants from the global majority. This pattern is apparent in policies from the Chinese Exclusion Act of 1882 through recent government actions offering expedited refugee status to White South Africans while aggressively detaining and deporting Latine, Black, Asian, and Middle Eastern people in the absence of due process and in violation of their legal right to be in the United States. While race is a construction, it has been and continues to be deployed in ways that have tremendous consequences for all of us.

As a White person with a still underdeveloped but growing understanding of race, it has been helpful for me to listen to perspectives of people of the global majority about how contested and mutable these categories are. At the end of this chapter, you can find a list of resources that have supported my growing understanding of race and racism. While race is an invention, as Menakem reminds us it has "teeth and claws" with the power to do harm. In teaching about race and racism in early childhood, we are seeking to defang the harmful reality of racial bias so that all of our children may thrive.

When I was younger, I thought as many of us do that racism is the same thing as disliking people whose racial or ethnic background differs from one's own. It has been important for me to recognize a definition of racism as the toxic combination of prejudice plus power. This definition reminds us that one individual's racial prejudice does not have the same consequences as the racism that has the power to shape policies and practices. Several years ago, I attended a parent workshop at my children's public elementary school about raising anti-racist children. The workshop was taught by the Center for Racial Justice in Education, and it expanded my understanding of racism and how it functions. The workshop facilitators offered us a framework for understanding that racism operates in three ways: as *internalized,* as *interpersonal,* and as *institutional.*

Internalized racism causes White people to absorb a false sense of superiority and leads people of all races to associate whiteness with greater value, as when people describe predominantly White schools as "good schools," and predominantly White neighborhoods as "good neighborhoods." Internalized racism can also cause people of the global majority to harbor the false idea that things associated with people with darker skin are of lower quality. We can see this in the colorism that lives in many diasporic communities. A person from India, or Guatemala, or Vietnam, or

Jamaica who has lighter skin often has more access to power and resources than a person with darker skin living in those places. Physical attributes associated with whiteness may be considered desirable. Hair that is straight and fine is called "good hair" (Norwood 2015; Walker 1983).

What does internalized racism look like in our schools? It looks like teachers of all races who describe White children as "smarter" or "better behaved" than children of the global majority. It looks like children of all races showing a preference for playing with White baby dolls or fighting over being able to play the roles of White superheroes and princesses in the dramatic play area (Sturdivant 2023).

Racism is also manifested in interpersonal dynamics. When my understanding of racism was less developed, it was *interpersonal racism* that most often came to mind. I thought of racism as what happens when someone crosses the street to avoid walking past a Black man, calls a Sikh man wearing a headscarf a terrorist, assumes a Latine person does not speak English, or refuses to get on a subway car filled with Asian American passengers due to anti-Asian hate stoked during a pandemic.

What does interpersonal racism look like in our schools? It looks like Black and Latine children being suspended or expelled for engaging in behavior that White children do with lesser consequences (Morris 2018; Noguera 2003). It looks like disproportionality in referrals to special education (Harry and Klingner 2022). It looks like a child with lighter skin refusing to hold hands with a child with darker skin because they believe dark skin is "dirty" or "ugly." If you doubt that such exchanges still occur, even in classrooms in New York City, you will be disheartened to learn in the coming chapters that instances of interpersonal racism are far too common.

Institutional racism is where the power that accompanies bias has the most broad-reaching impact. Banks have been documented to be less likely to offer home loans to people of the global majority as a function of institutional racism (Lutton, Fan, and Loury 2020), which in turn leads to the segregation in housing that contributes to a segregated system of schools (Hannah-Jones 2016). The system of mass incarceration imprisons people of the global majority at higher rates than White people for the same or lesser crimes, a function of institutional racism that has a consequence on the lives of many families (Alexander 2010; Stevenson 2014). The racial wealth gap in the United States is evident in findings from the Federal

Reserve in 2022 that "the typical White family had about six times as much wealth [$285,000] as the typical Black family [$44,900], and five times as much as the typical Hispanic family [$61,600]" (Aladangady et al. 2023). This disparity too is a symptom of institutional racism.

What does institutional racism look like in our schools? Institutional racism is visible in the long shadow that *de jure* or legal school segregation casts over schools today, many of which remain as segregated as they were when the historic *Brown v. Board of Education* case was decided in 1954 by the US Supreme Court, which decreed that separate is not equal (Rooks 2025). While school segregation is no longer legal, it remains a *de facto* condition that looks like White parents using coded language to describe schools that serve predominantly students of the global majority as "unsafe" and less desirable and choosing to concentrate White children in a handful of public schools (Hannah-Jones 2016). Institutional racism also results in the recent finding that "cost-adjusted spending in the average Black and Hispanic students' schools ranges from zero to 17.2% less than that in the average White students' schools" (Bifulco and Souders 2024).

Internalized, interpersonal, and institutional racism are all intertwined. A Black girl in the dramatic play area of our classroom might show a preference for dressing up as Anna or Elsa from the movie *Frozen* because she has internalized a sense that those characters are most desirable *and* because of the institutional racism in media that most often represents princess characters as White. As adults supporting young children's healthy racial identity development, it is important for us to consider the specific ways that racism is being manifested in our work so that we can understand the beliefs that undergird our actions. For example, if I notice that children of all races in my class are frequently fighting over who gets to play with the White baby dolls, I can make changes in my classroom to counteract this internalized racism. Because of institutional racism, children of all races most often see images of White characters as the default or standard in movies, books, advertising, and so on. As a teacher I might choose to counteract the effect of the proliferation of White characters by including many more images of people of the global majority in my classroom. I can review the images on posters around my room to make sure that they show babies and children of the global majority. I can make sure that I stock my classroom library with books that affirm the identities of children of the global majority.

When?

Many adults fear speaking to young children about race and racism, believing that early childhood is too soon to learn about these concepts. These adults may believe that young children do not notice race, and that by talking about it we are putting ideas in their heads. Research has demonstrated, however, that young children do observe race and that they absorb and internalize the harm caused by racism and the lie of White racial superiority (Husband 2012; Sturdivant 2023; Winkler 2009). Studies have found that children of all races show a preference for dolls with lighter skin and that their perception of who among their peers is well behaved, smart, or a good playmate is informed by race. If we wait too long to speak openly with young children about race, we have too much work to undo by the time we *think* children are old enough to talk about it.

Another common misconception is that teaching about race will make White children feel bad about themselves or guilty or ashamed. Many adults are afraid that teaching about race and racism has the potential to be traumatizing for young children of all racial identities. When early childhood teachers are adept and well prepared to teach and learn about race with young children, these fears are unrealized. This book will offer many examples of how early childhood educators have offered young children opportunities to learn about race and racism in ways that are affirming and that offer young children a sense of the power they have to make the world a more just and loving place. However, when educators are not yet well prepared to teach these topics with young children, harm can be done. Just because there is the possibility for educators to do this work poorly, this does not mean that we should not do it. Instead, it is essential that we give educators the training, support, and resources necessary to do this critical work well.

Children observe differences at a very young age. They also begin to absorb that these different identities have implications for how we live. Most people in the United States live in segregated communities. This is especially true for White people. Dr. Beverly Daniel Tatum, who has studied racial identity development extensively, has cautioned that children observe what we *do* about race even more than what we say. In a 2019 episode of National Public Radio's *Life Kit: Parenting* podcast entitled "Talking Race With Young Children," Tatum cautioned that while many White parents strive to communicate to their children that everyone is equal and that race does not matter, children observe that their parents choose to live in racially segregated communities. As Tatum noted,

> Seventy-five percent of White adults live in communities that are almost if not entirely White. And so the immediate surroundings offer little opportunity for direct engagement with other children of color, adults of color. And so much of the culture conveys messages that reinforce that separation.

We tell children that we are all equal, but they observe that we live separately and often have unequal access to resources because of race. For example, children may overhear us call a neighborhood unsafe and then observe that in the neighborhood we are describing most of the residents are people of the global majority. In our early childhood classrooms, we assert that everyone should be treated fairly and that we are all equally valued. Yet young children may notice that, because of teachers' unconscious bias, it is a Black boy who is most often reminded to use their walking feet while a White girl is most often praised for being ready on the rug. We owe it to our children to do better.

Throughout the time I was interviewing early childhood educators for this book, we were all aware of the culture war raging over the false assertion that kindergarteners were being indoctrinated in Critical Race Theory (CRT). Elections are being won and lost over the moral panic that this assertion elicits. Never mind that CRT is a complex concept with origins in legal scholarship that is never taught in any early childhood classroom. While the inaccurate use of terms like CRT is distracting, it masks very real and persistent resistance to the idea that children should be taught anything about race, especially in early childhood. Across the country White parents are turning up at school board meetings and are lobbying their elected officials to demand that race *never* be talked about in schools. Even aspects of curriculum that do not explicitly mention race, such as social and emotional curriculum that seeks to strengthen learners' capacity for empathy and perspective taking, are under attack as they are accused of serving as a Trojan horse for a radical racial justice curriculum. White adults who object to teaching about race argue that White children will be harmed or damaged by learning about the racist history of our country.

Additionally, what they are rarely saying aloud is that they fear this will lead to the loss of power and privilege for White people. Aside from this brief mention here, I will not go further in engaging the current debate, but it is important to recognize the context in which teachers are doing the courageous work of teaching and learning about race and racism with young children, despite very real threats to educators who do this work.

I offer this book to support my argument that all adults, especially early childhood teachers, have an obligation to support children's development of a healthy racial identity. If young children do not feel affirmed in their identities in school, they are only able to bring a part of themselves to the process of growing and learning. We cannot support children's healthy racial identity development—or indeed their development as a whole—if we are forbidden from talking about race and racism in our early childhood classrooms.

Where?

We are all on a lifelong journey to fully understand our identities. As we learn and grow, we gain knowledge about who we are as individuals, and we also understand how we fit into the context of the human family. Our understanding of our own personhood evolves with experience. Young children begin their journey of self-discovery in the context of home and family. Entering the early childhood classroom, they begin to learn who they are in the ever-widening context of community. In the field of early childhood education, we use the phrase *developmentally appropriate* to describe the ways that we create learning experiences for young children that they are ready to receive. We design curriculum that takes into consideration what we know about child development in general and also what we know about the specific group of children in our care. I believe much of the fear people have about addressing race and racism in early childhood classrooms comes from a concern that we will be teaching about these topics in a way that is not developmentally appropriate. No early childhood teacher would ever advocate for showing young children pictures of lynching, though the pervasiveness of that brutal violence is a historical truth in the United States. This may seem like an extreme example, but I want to name an unspoken fear some people may have when we talk about teaching and learning about race and racism in early childhood. I have written this book to document the powerful and varied ways that early childhood teachers can offer young children a developmentally appropriate experience in learning about race and racism. I hope that these examples will dispel some of the fears that those of us, especially those who do not spend time in early childhood classrooms, may hold.

While it is always important for early childhood educators to ensure their teaching is grounded in developmentally appropriate practices, we must avoid bringing our adult fears to bear in deciding whether children are ready to learn about race and racism. There are many adults who argue that teaching about race and racism in early childhood can never be developmentally appropriate practice. Yet the research shows us that in the absence of providing these opportunities for growth and learning, children begin to absorb racist messages at a very young age (Sturdivant 2023; Winkler 2009). Also vital is providing educational experiences that are *culturally sustaining* (Paris and Alim 2017). These are educational practices that affirm and uplift all children. Culturally responsive and sustaining practices allow all children to have their identities celebrated rather than negated, and this affirming learning environment creates the conditions that allow learners to thrive (Jones 2025; Ladson-Billings 1995; Paris and Alim 2017; Rose 2024).

By this point it should be clear that I advocate offering young children opportunities to learn about race and racism in all early childhood classrooms, and that we must do this work in ways that are both developmentally appropriate *and* culturally sustaining. In the rest of this book, I will share how early childhood educators I spoke with have approached this complex and generative work. I want to begin by telling you a little bit more about the educators I spoke with and the specific contexts in which they are all working.

The vast and varied field of early childhood is comprised of different program types that follow a range of educational philosophies. I sought to interview educators working in a variety of contexts, including Head Start, public and private schools, and programs serving children from birth through eight years old. Eleven of the educators I spoke with worked in public schools, ten worked in independent/private preschools, and six worked in Head Start or Early Head Start programs. Most of my interviews with the educators were one-on-one, though I also interviewed three teaching teams of two or three educators who worked together in the same classroom.

All educators, children, and schools in this book are referred to by pseudonyms. In New York City, many public schools are known by number (for example, P.S. 123), but since six different public elementary schools are mentioned in this book, I invented names for them (for example, the Kellman Public School) to avoid confusing readers with too many numbers. Tuition-based schools in New York refer to themselves as "independent" schools. However, in generating pseudonyms for these schools I have opted instead to use the term "private school." My use of the word "private" as an alternative to "independent" is intentional; I wish to highlight that schools that require payment of tuition are, by their nature, exclusionary (Gasoi and Meier 2017). While many of these schools have made substantial commitments to cultivating racial diversity among their student body, according to the Pew Research Center, historically schools that require families to pay tuition or request financial aid tend to be majority White institutions (Schaeffer 2024). Racist policies and practices (ranging from the institution of slavery to redlining and legacy admissions to elite schools) have produced the racial wealth gap (McGhee 2021) in the United States, ensuring that White families have been able to amass wealth while systematically and intentionally excluding families of people in the global majority. Even as private schools have sought to enroll students of the global majority, they rarely achieve enrollment that represents the racial diversity of our wider communities. This may only partially be explained by the cost barrier and might also reflect families' reluctance to send their children to a school where they will be in the minority.

While the professionals I interviewed taught in a variety of environments, they had one important thing in common. Nearly all worked in a school or program with a child-centered philosophy of education. All early childhood programs are necessarily oriented toward children's interests and needs. However, I chose to interview teachers in schools and programs that make a special effort to be child- and family-centered and that use an intentionally progressive approach to teaching and learning. Rather than following a script of purchased curricula, these educators have a strong hand in adapting and designing learning experiences that are responsive to what they know about the children in their classrooms.

In addition to finding educators who work in a variety of settings, it was important to me to speak with educators who describe themselves by a variety of racial identities. Educators' racial and other intersectional aspects of their identities—gender, class, religion, and so on—shape the lens through which they view their work with young children. At the start of every interview, I asked educators to share how they described themselves in terms of race and ethnicity. Labels such as those used in an official form or government census to describe race often fail to reflect the more nuanced ways we describe ourselves. In the coming chapters, I will offer biographical details from the educators' lives.

Notably, of the twenty-seven educators I interviewed, five identify as male, a proportion that is significantly higher than the percentage of male-identified teachers in the early childhood workforce as a whole. According to a 2023 report from the US Bureau of Labor Statistics, fewer than 4 percent of preschool teachers identify as male. The higher number of male teachers can be partly explained by the fact that the network of educators I reached out to for these interviews included participants in my previous study focused on the experiences of male-identified early childhood educators (Cole et al. 2019).

I began finding interviewees by reaching out to educators in my professional network, including several of my former students now working in the field. This approach to cultivating participants in this project was intentional. Many of the educators work in schools and classrooms I have visited many times, and I have observed them modeling an approach to teaching and learning that I believe nurtures young children's healthy growth and learning. My search extended to educators with whom I did not have a preexisting relationship, but who had been recommended to me by other interviewees or my colleagues as people who would have important ideas to offer to the conversation. The collection of stories about teaching in the following chapters is drawn from the experiences of a curated sample of educators whose practice holds great promise. It was my intention to amplify the voices of educators who are committed to doing this vital but often complicated work.

Why?

We live in a society where the dream of a just and loving world has not yet been realized. In our early childhood classrooms, we strive to model a community where everyone is treated fairly, where everyone gets what they need, and where we are all equally valuable and valued. However, when children step outside of our classrooms and, sadly, far too often even within our classrooms, they see evidence that contradicts these messages. If we are not actively counteracting negative messages about race, we leave children to inhale the smog of racism (Tatum 1997). We can interrupt children's absorption of these messages by providing learning experiences that celebrate all children's racial identities and cultures. We build young children's sense of themselves by affirming who they are. In our curriculum we must provide examples of people from all racial and ethnic identities living and thriving, doing ordinary and extraordinary things. In our curriculum we must provide examples of people of all identities who have fought to bring about a more just and loving world, so that our children can see themselves in that work. In a world that centers the perspectives and accomplishments of people who have been called White, we can make our classrooms spaces that elevate and celebrate all people.

Because we still live in a society that relies on the lie of white supremacy at the foundation, children who identify as White absorb a false sense of their own superiority. In order for white supremacy to persist, each generation needs to be socialized into believing the toxic and false narrative of white superiority. Interrupting this process is a responsibility of the adults in White children's lives in order to nurture their development of a healthy racial identity. Loving adults in young children's lives are responsible for their moral, social, and emotional development. If a child destroys another child's block construction, we help them to see that they have caused harm to another person. We find ways to help them take responsibility for repairing that harm. We work with them to think about what they could do differently going forward. If we allow young White children to internalize a sense of their own superiority, we are abdicating our responsibility to support their moral development. Supporting White children in understanding that all human beings are equally full of promise is an essential part of raising children who can be at home in their own bodies and in our multiracial, multicultural world and who will not leverage the power of their unearned privilege to oppress and harm others.

The early childhood classroom is a place where we can disrupt the lie of white supremacy, where children can have their identities seen, valued, and celebrated and where they can be invited to build a more just and loving world. I hope this book can be a resource for people engaged in this work. By considering portraits of teachers and narratives of their classroom practices, we can join in a conversation about what is needed to do this work well. We can commit to supporting ourselves and each other in continually growing to do this work better.

Coda: Who Am I?

Before I describe the work of the educators I interviewed, I must first acknowledge the complexity of my position as a White educator. I recognize that the way white supremacy works means I am often granted authority and power even when I may have done very little to earn it. Despite the presumption of expertise that I am often granted, I am well aware that on the topic of race I will always be a learner. I especially wish to recognize how I have relied on listening closely to people of the global majority as I seek to do better when it comes to teaching and learning about race and racism. Without wanting to burden people of the global majority with the responsibility to educate me about race and racism, I seek out all sources (books, podcasts, movies, and similar) that give me the opportunity to hear what a variety of people of the global majority have to say about race and racism. Learning from a variety of sources proves that the views on race of people of the global majority are as varied as individual human beings. The persistence of white supremacy relies on the willful ignorance of White people. There is evidence everywhere we look that racism and white supremacy do harm, and yet White people like me are encouraged to keep our heads in the sand. Knowing that my whiteness has protected me from learning about race and racism, I am continually engaged in a process of playing catch-up by listening to and learning from people of the global majority. This includes being self-reflective about seeing the impact of my own whiteness on my life and work. This learning is just a start, though, as White women like me participating in anti-racist book clubs has not yet led to the end of racism (Jackson and Rao 2022). Awareness must be paired with concrete action that works to confront and dismantle racist policies and practices.

I hope to offer this book in a spirit of humility about my own growth as a White educator who will be forever learning about race and racism. My primary goal in writing this book is to elevate and amplify the voices and perspectives of teachers as they engage in this complex, challenging, and often joyful work. This book is not a how-to manual. It offers examples of the ways that educators I have talked to have engaged in the messy work of teaching and learning about race and racism alongside young children. The work we do is always imperfect. This book is my invitation to other adults who want to consider the possibility that the ways we raise our children might bring us closer to creating a just and loving world. It is an invitation to invest in ourselves and in each other so that we can do this work well and so that when we are inevitably imperfect in our attempts, we reinvest in learning how to do better and repairing the harm we may have caused. This book is an invitation to be courageous and curious. Our children are ready for us to do this work. They need our support to grow up healthy and whole. We owe it to them to be ready.

> **Resources that support our ongoing learning about issues of race and racism in the United States**
>
> All My Relations *podcast*
>
> *National Public Radio's* Code Switch *podcast*
>
> *LAist's* Inheriting *podcast*
>
> Intersectionality Matters *podcast with Kimberlé Crenshaw*
>
> *Futuro Media's* Latino U.S.A. *podcast*
>
> *Scene On Radio's* Seeing White *podcast series*

Resources with a focus on race in education

Integrated Schools *podcast*

School Colors *podcast*

Lemonada Media's No One Is Coming to Save Us *podcast*

Teaching While White *podcast*

CHAPTER 2

How We Teach About Race

I try to be very conscious all the time that everything I do is being seen and being digested by small children. And that my main thing is that I want to speak love and trust and care inside all of these children. Those are the three pillars of my day.

—Jasmine, interview transcript

The academics are great, but if our kids are not being affirmed—I mean, it's tied to that, right? Our kids' success is tied to them being affirmed in our classrooms. It's super important. Because if they don't feel like what we're teaching is relevant to them or speaking to them, they're just going to zone out.

—Javier, interview transcript

Early childhood is a time when children come to know who they are. They observe how our identities influence the ways that we live in the world. Children come to understand their intersectional identities related to gender, race, culture, language, family diversity, religion, and other categories. They can understand that they may share one aspect of their identity in common with some of the people in their lives, but that some of their identifiers may be different. For example, a child whose family comes from the Dominican Republic may know that his best friend's *abuela* also comes from there, and may have observed that both families speak Spanish at home. But they also know that they have darker skin than their best friend and that their mother's favorite shirt reads "Proud Afro Latina."

The child also knows that their best friend has lighter skin and that their friend's family is called White. Children can hold all of these differences and similarities in their hearts and minds without judgment, without assigning greater value *or* diminishing anyone's identity. Bias is learned, not innate.

Every one of us deserves to feel affirmed and celebrated from birth through adulthood. We recognize the ways we are unique and we also notice the aspects of our identity that we share with others. For young children, coming to understand their identities should unfold through a healthy process that is supported by knowledgeable, trusted adults in their lives. Unfortunately, due to racism and other forms of bias, marginalization, and oppression, many young children receive and begin to absorb negative messages related to their own and others' identities at a very early age. White children receive and begin to absorb messages that offer the false assertion that our bodies have greater value, that we deserve access to more resources and power than people of other races. Children of the global majority receive and begin to internalize messages that people like them are less valuable and will receive less access to power and resources than people who are called White. Too early, many children of the global majority have to learn that because of racism their bodies are more likely to be harmed. If we begin to talk to children of all races early, we can provide them with a strong foundation to resist these messages of bias. This begins by creating spaces in our classrooms and in our homes that uplift and affirm all children's racial identities.

Research on how children begin to understand race and their own racial identities has demonstrated that young children begin to absorb messages about race at a very early age. They see that our world is organized in a way that sorts, categorizes, and assigns value to human beings on the basis of racial differences. While we must start young children's education about race by affirming and celebrating their identities, it is important for us to also teach young children about how racism and the false myth of white supremacy have been deployed to harm people. However, before we teach young children about racism, we must first invest in supporting their healthy racial identity development to offer them a strong foundation of loving themselves. In the next chapter, we will learn how early childhood educators tackle the challenging task of teaching young children about racism. In this chapter, we will learn how educators begin the process of supporting young children's understanding of what we mean when we talk about race and fostering their healthy racial identity development.

All children deserve to have their healthy racial identity development supported by the loving adults in their lives (Jones 2025). What does healthy racial identity development look like? It looks like children of the global majority, whose racial identities have been marginalized, continually receiving affirming messages about their identities. This is a baseline that is necessary to strengthen their resilience in the face of the negative messages they will inevitably receive about their identities. It is what is required to prevent children of the global majority from internalizing the toxicity of white supremacy. White children, whose racial identities have been privileged, need to continually receive clear messages that the color of their skin does not make them superior to any other person. They also need to understand the power they have to disrupt the process by which they are always granted privilege.

All children deserve to feel whole and to feel pride in themselves for exactly who they are. All children are born with the capacity to love themselves and others. Teaching children that people of every race deserve to feel whole and to feel pride in who they are helps children of the global majority to navigate living in a world that is not yet fully loving and just. Being honest with children about the ways that adults have used the invention of race to privilege some and oppress others does not negate White children's capacity to love themselves or prevent them from being able to celebrate and honor who they are. Rather, it allows them to celebrate and honor themselves fully and authentically. Being clear in reinforcing children's understanding that no person is inferior or superior because of their racial identity is part of our responsibility in supporting young children's moral development.

Conversely, when we allow White children to feel that the color of their skin makes them special or superior to people with different colored skin, we produce the conditions for them to act in immoral ways. This is the lie that enabled my White ancestors to steal land from the people who lived here before Europeans arrived. This is the lie that enabled my White ancestors to kidnap human beings from Africa and use enslavement and forced labor to build the economic foundations of the colonies that would become the United States. This is the lie that produces inequality in housing and education and disparities in health outcomes today. This is the lie that we must disrupt for our children to live in a just and loving world.

Designing Curriculum with Thought and Care

The early childhood educators I spoke with understand that affirming all children's healthy racial identity development is an essential component of their work. They demonstrated tremendous thought and care in designing curriculum that teaches about race in a way that is responsive to what they know about the children in their care. In the field of early childhood education, we know that our teaching must reflect *culturally sustaining* and *developmentally appropriate practice*, offering opportunities for learning that the children in our care are ready to receive. When teaching and learning with young children about race, teachers can draw on promising practices and curricula developed by other educators, but we base our teaching choices on what we know about child development and about the particular experiences and development of the children in our care. Skilled educators always adapt curricula to be responsive to what they know about the children in their classrooms.

When we think about designing learning experiences for young children, we often begin by considering their age and what experiences have contributed to their growth and learning to date. Teachers of very young children, birth through age three, know that they must be intentional in designing a classroom environment that serves as a medium for learning. Philosophies related to young children and their learning have been offered by scholars such as Maria Montessori, who described the school environment as playing the very active role of another teacher in the classroom. Early childhood educators provision for very young children to learn about race by ensuring that the materials in their classroom offer representations of people of all different races. Zara, who identifies as Indian American and Guyanese, and who teaches children from birth to age two at an Early Head Start program, explained: "Because they're young, we focus mainly on picture books and wordless books. We also have different-colored baby [dolls] and books with different-colored people." Shu Wen, who identifies as Chinese, works with two- to three-year-olds at the same program as Zara, which is located in New York City's Chinatown in Lower Manhattan. She and her colleagues take care to display pictures throughout the classroom that depict people of all different races. Shu Wen and her colleagues are also intentional about selecting books for their classroom library. She explains: "We try to choose more culturally inclusive books, more different faces they're going to see. So it's not just White people or White babies that you are going to see on those books."

Shu Wen is fortunate to be teaching in a time when the field of children's literature has grown in addressing issues of racial representation. The University of Wisconsin–Madison's Cooperative Children's Book Center's (CCBC) completes an annual review of representation in children's literature. In 2024 the center found that, for the first time in its annual review of children's books published that year, just over half (51 percent) featured a protagonist that was a person from the global majority (Cooperative Children's Book Center 2025). This means there are many options available now for early childhood teachers who wish to stock their libraries with high-quality children's literature representing a diversity of races and cultures. Vivian, who identifies as Chinese American and was raised in Vietnam, teaches in the same center as Zara and Shu Wen. She emphasized that having diverse classroom libraries is a shared priority of all her colleagues at the center. She explained, "Our school classroom always has inclusive books. Even though we're predominantly Chinese . . . there's also Black and Hispanic. So that's the setting here. But we always have books."

Literacy scholar Rudine Sims Bishop coined the term "windows and mirrors" to describe the importance of having early childhood classroom libraries that reflected a diversity of experiences (Sims Bishop 1990). Sims Bishop emphasized that young children need to be able to see themselves reflected or mirrored in the faces of characters in the books that they encounter. Children of all races also need to have books that offer "windows" or "sliding glass doors" that allow them to observe other lives and experiences and empathize with people different from themselves. Prekindergarten public school teacher and early childhood teacher educator Candice, who identifies as African American and Native American, thoughtfully considered the importance of filling her bookshelves with diverse books. She explained:

> Not only do your children of color need to see themselves in books, children who are White need to see those books too. Because they're going to say, "Oh, there can be a princess that doesn't actually look like me." Or, "Wait. Black people own homes and they go to sleep in beds at night." These are

things that, if you don't see it, as a child you might not realize it actually exists. So I think, not only do children need to be represented in books, so they see themselves, but other children need to see diversity in books so that they learn the tolerance and they just know by osmosis, "This is a reality. This happens too. We can see this." And I think as they learn that when they're younger, as they move up that reality, that little seed is in them. So when they face something that they say, "That's not fair," they can notice and say, "This is not the way it's supposed to be."

Candice sees the project of providing diverse books in her classroom as a vital component of her work in supporting her students' healthy racial identity development. She wants all children to know that every possibility is available to every child. Children's literature can serve as a vehicle for young children to see possibilities that might not yet exist in reality, or at least realities that they have not yet been exposed to in their lives. Most of us live in racially segregated communities, so children's literature offers us the opportunity to step into the life experiences of people who are different from us. It allows us to gain knowledge of and respect for the ways that we may live differently and also to feel connections with people who may look different but have the same needs, fears, and dreams.

Sapphire, who identifies as Black, and Eliza, who identifies as White and Jewish, teach three-year-olds at the Emilia Private School. Like Candice and many other early childhood teachers, they draw on the increasingly rich collection of children's literature that addresses race as they teach and learn with their students. However, if Sapphire and Eliza are not able to find a book that addresses the exact topic they want to discuss with the children, they turn to the practice of creating their own books that then become a part of the classroom library. For example, the teachers created a book that they titled *What Do You Call the Color of Your Skin and What Would You Like Other People to Call It?* Their use of this book will be discussed more in the coming chapter on anti-racist classrooms. Designing customized educational materials requires a level of knowledge and skill to be done thoughtfully, but educators should not feel constrained if books that address the topics they wish to teach about do not yet exist.

Observing and Affirming Ourselves

The creation of self-portraits is another staple of early childhood curriculum. This process asks children to look closely at themselves and gives them the opportunity to celebrate the ways that they are the same as and different from one another. Completing and collecting self-portraits throughout the year also offers children the opportunity to see themselves grow and change. Lara, who identifies as White Italian American, is a pre-kindergarten teacher at the Green Public School. She sees the process of making self-portraits as an opportunity for deep learning about race. Lara integrates the study of living artists of a variety of racial identities into her curriculum. She also wants her students to experience their own capacity as art makers. When her class creates self-portraits, Lara includes opportunities for the children to learn about the science of color mixing as they create a paint color that matches their own skin and other attributes as accurately as possible—their own "skin-color recipe." She works with each child to use all of the primary colors to mix the color brown, and then add drops of black paint to add shade to the color or white paint to add tint. As they work, Lara poses questions that lead the children to observe themselves closely:

> "Okay, put your paintbrush to the skin. Is your skin a little lighter? Is it a little darker? Is it cooler, or warmer? What should we add?" And we make a recipe together so that they can keep it. . . . It's a huge thing where we're actually just focusing on our skin color, and we're all focusing on how our skin color is different.

Lara finds that the children become fascinated observing each other as they mix paints to discover their own skin-color recipe. Completing the process with each child in her classroom can take some time, but Lara finds it deeply worthwhile when she sees the attention the children bring to the process. She recalled, "What's really special about it is that it's one kid doing their skin color and there will always be five other kids who just want to sit there and watch." In this way, each child in the classroom has the opportunity to be seen and attended to fully by their peers. To support the children's understanding of what makes our skin different colors, Lara uses books like *All the Colors We Are: The Story of How We Get Our Skin Color* by Katie Kissinger. She appreciates that the book "talks about melanin and talks about how we're all different shades of brown, even though we use race words like White and Black." The children continue their self-portraits by using hand mirrors to observe the shapes of their eyes, noses, and lips, as well as the texture, color, and length of their hair. When the portraits are complete, Lara hangs them in the classroom. She noted: "[It's] really rewarding for the kids to see all their portraits up next to each other and really look at how they're different and they're similar. But also . . . it's special that they're all different."

Candice, who teaches prekindergarten at the Kellman Public School, also sees the process of making self-portraits as an opportunity for children to find joy and affirmation in their differences. Though she does not include a color mixing study with her class, Candice noted that her children bring great attention to selecting colors that most closely match their skin tone from a selection of multicultural paints. When the children complete their self-portraits, the class enjoys a gallery walk to appreciate each child's painting. The children engage in this activity with joy and interest in each other, and Candice observes, "They don't feel like it's a bad thing to have a different tone. It's just a different tone." Similarly, Javier, who identifies as White and Latino, teaches prekindergarten at La Casa Public School where he addresses the topic of skin color in his teaching. He and his co-teachers have developed curriculum that focuses on learning about the human body. As part of this study the educators read books that explain the science of skin color. These books educate the children about how different amounts of melanin in our skin produce different skin tones for each of us. Having clear explanations for how our differences in skin color, hair texture, and facial features have evolved is extremely helpful to young children as they grow in their understanding of the world.

The Classroom Community as a Source of Emergent Curriculum on Culture

Every early childhood teacher knows that young children are especially interested in learning about themselves and the people around them.

There are many ways to incorporate a study of ourselves and others into the early childhood curriculum that supports children in celebrating their own identities and in respecting the identities of others. Audre, who identifies as African American and Native American, teaches in a multi-age classroom with three- to five-year-olds at Grasshopper Montessori Private Preschool. Montessori curriculum traditionally incorporates the study of global cultures, and Audre begins by designing her curriculum as a study of the heritage of the teachers and families in the room. She explains, "We study each other. We'll study my background and where I came from, and the kids will ask questions. And then we'll study somebody from Ireland. And we just go around the classroom." Colette, who identifies as Grenadian and Black, Hannah, who identifies as White, and Jordana, who identifies as Brazilian and White, are a team of teachers who work in another classroom at Grasshopper Montessori. Like Audre, they capitalize on the cultural knowledge of the extended classroom community to design learning experiences. Bringing the knowledge that families hold into the classroom serves to build connections between home and school and offers children the opportunity to learn about themselves and others.

When I was a child, the holidays celebrated in school were largely Christian holidays. Because this approach was not inclusive of all cultural traditions, some educators have responded by avoiding discussion of any holidays. Prekindergarten teacher Jasmine, who identifies as Guyanese, teaches with Lara at the Green Public School. She sees learning about the heritage and traditions of the children in her classroom as a tremendous opportunity for her students to see themselves reflected in the curriculum. Jasmine explained:

> I don't want to keep holidays out of my classroom. I want to welcome them. But I make sure that if I read about one holiday, I'm going to read about them all. And [I find] books about each and every holiday that is celebrated in my class, and holidays that are not celebrated in my class, to recognize those who aren't a part of our room.

For some educators, teaching about the experiences and culture of people of racial and cultural backgrounds different from their own can feel challenging. Montessori preschool teacher Hannah acknowledged that it can feel complicated for her to speak about the traditions of people who are different from her. She reflected candidly:

> We tend to focus more on culture than on race. Recently for Chinese New Year, [a student's] grandmother came in to talk with us and shared some artifacts and information. Last year a Jewish mother of one of our students came in to talk about how their family celebrated Hannukah. Things like that, where we can. But honestly, that's been uncomfortable. Like a couple of years ago, our only Chinese teacher wasn't here that year, and I talked about Chinese New Year, but it was in this form of, "Some people, if they are in China or from China, this is what they do." But it was just because I'm reading this page, and this is not something that I am at all truly familiar with. Like, this is deeply uncomfortable. I want to talk about it, because it's an interesting thing and it may affect children. As far as race, no, there isn't really anything particular in the curriculum or in our themes. It's more about—(Colette, Hannah's co-teacher, interjects: "It's more about culture.") Yeah, culture. It's about trying to make representation in our library. And about how we talk about each other.

At other points in our interview, it was clear that Hannah has grappled with the implications of her whiteness and knows that it is important that she and her co-teachers allow children of all races to have their identities affirmed in their classroom. Nonetheless, the tension and discomfort that Hannah expressed is shared by other early childhood educators. As we know, 80 percent of the education workforce are White like me and Hannah. We clearly need to support the development of a workforce that is reflective of the diversity of the children and families we educate. Concurrently, we must prepare teachers of all races to grow in their knowledge and also to develop the stance of cultural humility (Tervalon and Murray-García 1998) necessary to incorporate the experiences of people different from ourselves into our curricula. If White teachers feel unprepared or uncomfortable teaching about the culture and identity of people who are different from us, many children will miss out on the opportunity to have their identities visible in the classroom and to learn about the experiences and perspectives of those who are different from them.

Teacher Identity and Embodied Practice

Some of the teachers I spoke with shared how their own embodied racial identity provides young children with the opportunity to learn about race. Alvin, who identified as African American, was a retired teacher of two-year-olds. (Since our interview, Alvin has died, but his work continues to inspire me and all who knew him.) Alvin shared that, though he never named race explicitly in his classroom, he joined with children on their journey of noticing racial differences. Alvin taught for several decades at the Beekman Private School, which, like many other private schools in New York City, is predominantly White. Alvin was often the only person of the global majority in his classroom. His students were two-year-olds who had not yet learned that it can be impolite to express curiosity about people's bodies. Alvin reflected that his students often shared their observations and questions about the differences they observed between his body and theirs. When I asked Alvin to speak about how he addressed race in his teaching, he recalled:

> In my classroom children would often—when I would bend over to help them or tie their shoe or do something—they would often touch my hair and say, "Your hair is so different from mine, and it's so soft." And that would often lead to a conversation about sameness and difference. And it was kind of framed that way in our discussions. And so it was sort of indirectly addressing race on that level, but the word *race* at that age never really came up.

Alvin extended a great deal of generosity to the White children in this classroom in how he received their touching of his hair. It is important to acknowledge that when White people touch Black people's hair it is often without consent. While the intent on the part of the White person may be framed as innocuous, we need to recognize that this gesture hearkens back to the not-so-distant, violent history in our country when White people believed the lie that we could have ownership over Black bodies. Alvin, however, did not assign any malice to the children in his classroom when they reached up to touch his hair. Knowing two-year-olds intimately as he did, Alvin saw this as a natural expression of a two-year-old's way of making sense of the world, of learning through their senses, including touch. Early childhood educators have a role to play in instilling in young children their responsibility to seek consent and respect the boundaries that each person sets on their own body. But Alvin welcomed these gestures as an opportunity to join with children in their discovery of our differences.

Like the other teachers of children under three I interviewed, Alvin chose not to name race in his classroom. Yet he described the ways that he addressed the diversity of race and culture through his very presence as an African American male teacher in the classroom, drawing upon his own ways of expressing his identity as material for the curriculum of the class. A former church pianist and professional dancer, Alvin reflected,

> I guess I didn't directly address race, but the fact that I was an African American male with mostly White students, they basically saw what I did in the classroom as coming from somebody who didn't really look like them. That served as a model that, number one, males could be as caring as females for young children. And that a Black, African American male could also do that in the classroom whose skin color was in many cases somewhat darker than theirs.
>
> What I brought to the classroom was something that I deeply cared about as part of my self-expression, much of which took the form of music. And within the realm of music, playing a lot of folk songs and American folk songs that children would immediately grab onto and love and understand. And I was also playing piano. I had a lap Casio piano that I played daily, and we sang, oh yes! Singing was one way to build community. I mean, all of this is coming out of my church experience and my African American experience.
>
> And so without directly stating it in words, you sort of live it as part of the environment of the classroom. And as they learn through their senses, they experience it in their bodies, and then they began to understand that this is a primary way to be part of a group and to develop group connections and to

understand connections with others. And I think without directly saying it, because they connected to me, because I was the resource for it, they could see that, "Oh you can connect with a Black person this way, you can connect to anybody."

Other teachers reflected on the way that their very embodied presence in the classroom was in and of itself an opportunity for young children to learn about race and being in multiracial communities. This was particularly observed by teachers who worked in teaching teams comprised of teachers of different races. Precious, who identifies as African American and Native American, and Esperanza, who identifies as Mexican, teach three- and four-year olds together at the Family First Early Head Start program. They reflected on how their collaboration in the classroom offers their students an important model. They described referring explicitly to their own race, ethnicity, and racial differences when responding to issues that children raise related to race, recounting an incident when Annabella, the only White child in the classroom, made a racist remark. This will be explored in more detail in the next chapter on teaching about racism. Precious shared that in responding to the incident, she drew the children's attention to the race and ethnicity of everyone in the classroom, including Esperanza and herself, explaining:

> We talked about Ms. Esperanza coming from Mexico. We talked about me being Native American. We talked about other children who come from Caribbean. We talked about Annabella's parents coming from Italy. We talked about the texture of hair, different colors of hair. Different colors of eyes. Different complexions. And then we sat and we talked about our differences.

By naming and describing their own racial identities and differences, Precious and Esperanza modeled for the children the language we can use to talk about race and racial differences and ways to express an understanding of their own identities.

Lucely, who identifies as Latina, works as an assistant teacher in a Head Start classroom. She observed that the children in her class learn about race in part through being part of a multiracial community. She shared that during the All About Me unit at the beginning of the year, the teachers describe their own racial attributes as a way of noticing and affirming difference. Lucely explained:

> We bring the different shades, skin tone crayons, skin tone colors, and we bring different kinds of books. The teachers are coming from different countries. There can be a teacher from where I am from that is a different color from me. So, just the real life, hands-on experience, like, "Hey, this person's from here, but you see they have different colors and different hair texture." I would say we do this hands-on because my kids are small.

While many teachers use children's literature to open a conversation about racial differences, teachers like Lucely who are part of a multiracial teaching team and classroom community can offer children concrete experiences of understanding difference through speaking explicitly about differences in their classroom community. For very young children, this learning through direct experience may be the most concrete and meaningful, which is yet another argument for working toward more integrated schools.

Following Children's Observations and Questions

One thing we know about young children is that their process of making sense of the world involves asking a lot of questions. Early childhood educators who follow children in their inquiry can be assured of an engaging learning experience. In addition to developing planned curriculum to support young children's understanding of race, teachers must be ready to join with children in the moment as they share their observations and questions about race. For teachers who do not already have a comfort or fluency with talking about race this can feel intimidating. Many adults have been conditioned not to talk about racial differences, so it can feel overwhelming when children speak explicitly about what they notice. It also takes practice to be able to discern what exactly is behind children's observations and questions, how much they already know, and how much new information they are ready for. As with how we respond to all children's questions about complex topics (such as death or where babies come from), we can start by asking more questions to learn more about what they want to know. Early childhood educators sit alongside of young children as they construct meaning, offering new information when children seem ready.

Matthew, who identifies as Haitian American, worked at La Casa Public School but not as a classroom teacher. Instead he served in a community-building role that included strengthening the school's capacity to serve as an anti-racist institution. In this role he visited classrooms to support the teachers and got to know the children and how they are making sense of the world. Matthew described a series of interactions he has had with a six-year-old boy named Rahui whose family recently migrated to the United States from Mexico. Rahui had a friend named José who was Afro-Latino. Matthew described José's skin color as similar to Rahui's but noted that "his other features are Afro," adding that he wears his hair in braids. Every week when Matthew visited the classroom, he had a version of the following exchange with Rahui:

> Every week when [Rahui] sees me, he tells me, "Did I ever tell you, you look like José's dad?" And I say, "Me? I look like José's dad?" He says, "Yeah." I say, "Why do you think I look like José's dad?" And I don't think he had the words to say, "You both look Black." But he was just like, "You look like José's dad." And then I told him, "You know, I met José's dad. You know, José's dad actually looks more like you than he looks like me." He was like, "No!" He was like, "No way!" I said, "Yeah." But lo and behold, every week: "Matthew, you know you look like José's dad?" And so . . . I'm just letting his curiosity build. Because again, he hasn't added any value, he hasn't put any value on difference, it just catches him. So I'm kind of curious to see where this goes.

Matthew could tell that Rahui was engaging with him about these questions of identity as a way of making sense of his observations that his friend José is both racially similar to him and also different. If another adult asked Matthew, one of the only Black adults in the school, week after week if he was related to an Afro-Latino child, Matthew might take offense. However, he knew that these questions were part of Rahui's process of sense-making. He welcomed Rahui's questions with humor and his own curiosity and asked questions to better understand how Rahui was processing the new information he was absorbing. Matthew clarified that if a child shared something that could be harmful to themselves or others, he would be ready to intervene. He knows that children do receive and absorb negative messages about race and that they need support to know how these messages can be hurtful. He explained:

> There are comments that are malicious. Even if malice is not intended by the kid, it could just be something they learned from their parents or TV or whatever. So if someone says their hair is ugly, their nose is ugly, it's comments like that that we need to be more direct about. We're not engaging that. We could explore, "Why you think that?" or "Where did that come from?" But that's behavior that we're trying to nip in the bud. But if it's comments like, "Hey, I noticed—" We welcome the curiosity, because they're young children. They haven't said black is bad or dark is bad and light is good. They're just saying "Whoa! There is dark and there is light. What is this phenomenon of skin shade and hair texture that I'm discovering?"

As educators prepare themselves to respond to these teachable moments, it is important to be able to discern when children are simply noticing differences versus when they may have internalized a sense that there is a value assigned to differences. Children of all races may internalize messages that features of whiteness are desired and features of people of the global majority are less desirable. When we hear these values articulated, it is important to intervene. However, when a child is simply noticing difference, we can join with them as they use these observations to grow in their knowledge of the world.

Ewan, who identifies as White with Scottish and French/Irish parents, is a teacher to four-year-olds working at St. William Private Preschool. Ewan described the school, located in an affluent, predominantly White neighborhood, as "the first step into the Ivy League educational process." He shared his recollection of a conversation he had with one of his students who is South Asian. He described,

> She has darker skin, and she was talking about how her skin was darker than some other students. And I was like,

"Yeah, that's true." And I always frame questions. I said, "What do you think about that?" Or like, "How does that make you feel?" Or, "Have you noticed anything else that's different?"

Ewan posed questions to elicit more information about what the child was observing, but he also offered the opportunity for the child to share if she had any feelings associated with her observation that her skin color was different from that of many of her classmates. Recognizing that a four-year old may not yet be able to articulate their feelings about being one of the only people who shares her racial or ethnic identity in a community, Ewan was attentive to the possibility that this experience could be isolating.

Many adults hold the misconception that when we talk about race with young children we will be exposing them to content that is too mature for them to process and that has the potential to traumatize. As I hope you have seen illustrated in the examples above, teaching young children about race is distinctly different from teaching young children about racism. Teaching about race is an opportunity for each child to feel seen and whole and affirmed in our classrooms. We still do need to teach young children about racism, as it is our responsibility to make space for them to process the things they observe in the world that are inequitable and harmful. In the next chapter, we will explore how educators can teach about racism in ways that are culturally sustaining and developmentally appropriate for the children in their care. However, before we address the topic of racism, it is critically important for children of all races to have their identities affirmed in their classrooms. This is especially true for children who receive negative messages about their racial identities. As Matthew explained, "I think before you tell a Black kid that their ancestors have experienced oppression, it might be nice to tell that Black kid, 'Your skin is beautiful! Your hair is beautiful! Here is the beautifulness of the history of your people and the things that they have done.'"

I hope that the examples above have provided inspiration for how we can offer all young children the opportunity to celebrate themselves, to feel seen and whole and affirmed. Establishing a strong foundation of affirmation, self-love, and appreciation for others will give them the grounding necessary to join us in making the world a place that recognizes the full humanity of every one of us.

CHAPTER 3

How We Teach About Racism

It's different to be someone who's learning about racism than to be someone who experiences racism. And it's a privilege to be someone who's just learning about it.

—Lara, interview transcript

A number of years ago, my son's kindergarten teacher, Diandra Verwayne, (not a pseudonym) shared an anecdote from her classroom with me. Diandra and I had worked together on the school's Diversity Committee for several years before my younger child was a student in her class. It can be extremely difficult for parents and teachers to have frank and vulnerable discussions about anything, especially across the space of different racial identities. Diandra is Caribbean American, having migrated to New York City from Guyana as a child. In my experience I have observed that far too often White and economically privileged parents like myself wield our power and privilege in ways that disrespect educators (Cole 2016). I am always aware of the fact that as White parent and a teacher educator, I am responsible for continually working to earn the trust of educators and to communicate my deep respect for their knowledge. This is especially true in my relationships with educators who are people of the global majority. In order for us to have any kind of authentic and vulnerable exchange of ideas, I need to listen for the ways that I will inevitably make missteps, receive feedback with humility, and work to do better going forward. Because we had several years of working together at the school before I was a parent in her classroom, Diandra and I had gotten to know each other's perspectives. While we didn't always see eye to eye on every issue, we had a deep mutual respect, and I believe we had developed a degree of trust between us. From this foundation, we engaged in an ongoing conversation where we spoke openly and at length about issues related to race and racism and how these issues played out in our school community.

During the course of these conversations, Diandra shared the following story with me. One day when her kindergarten class returned from recess, Diandra could immediately tell that something was off in the classroom community. Several children rushed to tell Diandra that Tasha, an African American child, had told a group of children on the playground "I don't like White people." Several of the White children in the class who considered Tasha a friend expressed their distress. Though it was time for a math lesson to start, Diandra knew the children's attention would be preoccupied by this incident until they had time to process it. She sat the children in a circle and used Responsive Classroom strategies to give the children a chance to share what was in their hearts. She acknowledged that Tasha might have said what she said at recess because sometimes some White people have done things that harm Black people. She asked the class to share whether they had felt hurt by anything in their interactions in the classroom. Diandra reinforced an anti-bias message, explaining that even though some people of a particular race might do bad things, that does not mean we can conclude that this is true of all people of that race. Having had the chance to process this incident, the class moved on to their math lesson for the day.

In recounting the story to me, Diandra acknowledged that she was initially stunned and uncertain about how to respond. Nonetheless she knew that moving along with her day's lessons without giving the class a chance to learn and grow from this teachable moment was not an option. I know many teachers who, feeling unprepared to deal with such an incident with the nuance and complexity it warrants, would likely have either ignored the issue or chided Tasha with a hollow reprimand, "That's not a nice thing to say. We're all friends here." Diandra shared that this incident occurred during a time when the police killing of yet another unarmed Black person was in the news, and recognized that Tasha had likely overheard the phrase "I don't like White people" from one of the grown-ups in her life. She saw that this incident offered the class the opportunity to explore the problem of bias and prejudice, and to reinforce the idea we cannot paint all people of a race with a broad brush based on the harmful actions of some people.

Over the course of my conversations with other early childhood educators, I have heard different versions of this incident—a child of any race expressing that they will not hold hands with, do not want to play with, or find a problem with another person because of the color of their skin. Many early childhood educators, especially White teachers who lack the fluency to speak about race, feel incapable of responding to moments like this in their classrooms. They may claim that such exchanges do not happen, or when they do happen, they respond in an oversimplified, generic manner that does more harm than good (for example, "That's not nice"). Some courageous early childhood educators decide not to sweep such incidents under the rug. They make space, as Diandra did, to process what is happening with children, to address the harm caused, and to reinforce an anti-bias message.

When Tasha told her classmates, "I don't like White people," part of what she was communicating was fear. She was telling us that she has been traumatized by race-based violence against Black people. She was telling us she learned that a person who looks like her and her family was killed by the police, which contradicts the message we often tell children in school that police are here to protect us and keep us safe. And, as she was most likely repeating something overheard from the grown-ups in her life, she was also communicating that her family has been traumatized by this violence. Such knowledge and experiences might make Tasha wonder if she needs to be afraid of her White classmates.

When we assert that everyone is kind, when we fail to acknowledge that people of the global majority *are* harmed by racism, we are asking children, particularly children of the global majority, to believe in a world they can see with their own eyes does not yet exist. When we deny the reality of racism, they are right to distrust us. When we respond to incidents of racism, we need to acknowledge the harm that racism causes as we work with children to build a more equitable world in the future. To do that, teachers must understand how racism functions and be able to talk about it in ways young children can understand and that will not cause more harm. What follows are examples of how teachers address racism in their teaching, both through their planned curriculum and in response to incidents that arose in their classrooms.

In addressing how racism causes harm, it is helpful to borrow from the field of restorative justice. Restorative justice refers to a set of practices that emerged from the criminal and juvenile legal system. These practices have roots in Indigenous knowledge and approaches to building community and resolving conflict. The word "restore" refers to the goal of fostering healing and restoring a sense of community when harm has occurred. Schools have used restorative justice to move away from a top-down, authoritarian approach to discipline, instead using circle processes in which all parties have a voice in identifying appropriate consequences and actions that can be taken to repair harm. For healing circles to work, the community must first invest the majority of their time and energy in building healthy, trusting, respectful relationships. This foundational work of building community is referred to as Tier 1 work. If this foundation has not been laid, the higher-tier processes to address harm and conflict cannot succeed. If trust, respect, and relationship have not been cultivated, there is no healthy state for the community to be restored to.

Borrowing from the practices of restorative justice, we might consider that our Tier 1 work is providing young children with a strong foundation of their understanding of race, through supporting their own healthy racial identity development and by fostering in each child a deep appreciation for people with racial identities different from their own. Investing in this process then creates a foundation for teaching about racism. Racism and white supremacy do harm. By providing young children with a strong base, we help set them up with the knowledge, confidence, and resilience necessary to reckon with the painful legacy of racism in our past and in our present.

Planned Curriculum

The teachers I spoke with found children's literature to be an invaluable resource for introducing racism in way that young children can understand and engage with. Lola, who identifies as Mexican and Jamaican, teaches kindergarten at the racially diverse Kellman Public School. One year, she designed a unit of curriculum around the story of Ruby Bridges, the six-year-old child who was the first Black student at a segregated White school in New Orleans in 1960. Lola's class read and discussed multiple children's books about Ruby, watched a related movie, and recited a poem about her experiences for the Black History Month assembly. Lola's students connected deeply with Ruby Bridges because, unlike many other heroes of the civil rights movement, she was a young child like themselves. She recalled, "It was a very powerful thing, and the kids connected so much with that."

Lola shared how the children's interest in this piece of history led them to take the story home to share with their families. She recalled:

> The thing that I found so amazing was that they went home and they were telling their parents about Ruby Bridges. And many of the parents didn't even understand or know who Ruby Bridges was. So they were teaching their parents about her and what she did. You don't realize how much they learn and how much they can take with it.

Lola was struck by how deeply engaged her students were in this study and how they took pride in teaching their families about what they had learned.

Many teachers I spoke with used children's books to teach about the civil rights movement. However, they recognized a need for balance in the stories. If the only figure that children learn about is Martin Luther King Jr. and they learn that he was killed, they might conclude that fighting for justice is deadly. It is important for children to learn about people who have fought for justice and have lived and thrived. They must also understand that our work is not done. Ruth, who identifies as White and Jewish, reflected on her experiences as a new teacher working in the 1980s in de facto segregated schools serving primarily Black students. When reading children's books about the civil rights movement, Ruth observed that the books framed the fight for racial justice as a thing of the past. She recalled,

> I would read these books, and at the end of every kids book about Martin Luther King would be, "And now we're all together and it's all over." So every book ends with "And now we're all together." And I would look around the classroom and be thinking, "Oh, we're not all together."

While it is important for children to learn our history and to be inspired by examples of people who have fought for justice and equity, we cannot treat the history of injustice as a problem that has been solved. When we engage children in discussion of the work that we have left to do, we have the opportunity to invite them to join us in taking action to bring about change.

Javier, who identifies as Latino and White, teaches prekindergarten at La Casa Public School. He has also read a collection of biographies about Ruby Bridges with his class. He shared that throughout this unit the children ask questions, like, "Why did that happen? Why would they be mean to her?" This led Javier to wonder how far back to go in describing the racist foundations of the United States. When we spoke, he was not teaching his class about the history of the enslavement of Black people in this country, but he wondered about how to provide context for his children to understand why Ruby Bridges was treated unfairly because of the color of her skin. To support this dialogue I gave Javier a copy of a children's book that had just been published the month before our interview. The book is called *Our Skin: A First Conversation About Race* by Megan Madison and Jessica Ralli. Madison has worked extensively in professional development to train early childhood teachers in supporting the healthy development of young children in all aspects of their identities. Madison and Ralli, a children's librarian, developed a series of beautifully illustrated and thoughtfully researched books called First Conversations that open up discussions about race, gender, and consent, and that meet young children where they are. I shared with Javier the pages from *Our Skin* that address the origins of racism. The text reads:

> A long time ago, way before you were born, a group of white people made up an idea called race. They sorted people by skin color and said that white people were better, smarter, prettier, and that they deserve more than everybody else. That isn't true or fair at all! But it's a story that has been told for a long time. (Madison and Ralli 2021)

Books like *Our Skin* can respond to children's questions about the history of racism in this country, a history that still casts a shadow over our lives today. As we introduce specific figures and movements in the fight for racial justice, it is important to give children the information and tools to see these moments in history in a larger context.

In addition to teaching young children about the history of racism in the United States, teachers can activate young children's innate sense of fairness and offer them hands-on opportunities to discuss how bias based on difference produces harm for individuals and communities. Candice, who identifies as African American and Native American, teaches pre-kindergarten at the Kellman Public School. She has developed an activity for her class to experience the inherent injustice in resources being allocated only to some people as a result of a physical characteristic. Candice begins by reading and discussing the Dr. Seuss book *The Sneeches and Other Stories*. She acknowledges that some of Seuss's early work included racist imagery, but she still sees value in some of his work as a vehicle for teaching lessons about fairness and bias. *The Sneeches* is a story in which groups of characters fall in and out of favor depending on whether they have a star on their belly. After reading and discussing the book, Candice and her class are ready to move on to center time, when the children work independently with toys and materials throughout the room. While she is reading, Candice has asked her assistant teacher to set up materials in two different configurations. At one cluster of tables there are new boxes of crayons, large sheets of paper, and sharpened pencils. At another cluster of tables, the children see broken crayons, crumpled scrap paper, and pencils missing tips. On this day, Candice varies the process for dismissing children to select their materials. She walks around the meeting area and hands out star stickers to a random assortment of children. She then explains that the children with the stars can work at the tables with the fresh new materials, and directs the children without stars to the tables with the remnants. The children without stars notice the inequity immediately and begin to protest. Candice recounted, "They're like, 'That's not fair!' And I'm like, 'Why? Did you have a star?'" Each year as she offers this learning experience, Candice is moved when she observes that some of the children with stars offer materials to their friends without stars. Nonetheless, she can immediately feel the children's sadness, anger, and discomfort brewing in the room, so she quickly halts the experiment and brings the children back to the carpet to debrief. She begins by asking the children, "Why is everybody looking so grumpy?" The children respond, "Because it's not fair!" So Candice offers the class the opportunity to take action to solve the injustice. She asks, "Well, what should I do?" The children retort,

> "We're not Sneeches! You see how silly that man was. Everybody's the same, whether they have a star or not." And I'm

like, "Really?" And then I have the ones with the stars come up and I'm like, "Here. Give a star to somebody." So they all give stars to the other kids that didn't have the stars, and then we really have the good center time with the new crayons and I bring out some new toys that we didn't have before. So everybody's happy.

An experienced educator, Candice has thought deeply about how to teach about inequality in a way that her students will be able to engage with. She is also aware of the potential of such lessons, when done poorly, to cause more harm. Teachers who offer children hands-on experiences or the opportunity to role-play stories of injustice must be extremely careful and conscious to not offer these lessons in a way that might amplify racial trauma. For example, many of us have heard about teachers who assign children of color to play the role of enslaved people in reenacting periods of history. Obviously that approach to teaching about race and racism is harmful and should not be used in any classroom. However, children often find learning most memorable when they have a direct rather than passive experience of concepts such as justice and equality. When handled well, these kinds of learning experiences can be transformative in producing children who will speak up in the face of injustice.

Supporting Young Children's Understanding of Events in the World

In addition to designing curriculum that gives children hands-on experiences, Candice prepares herself to respond to how children are processing news of injustice in the world. The Kellman Public School is not far from one of the main gathering points for protests that occurred in the wake of the killing of George Floyd and Breonna Taylor by police in 2020. Marches starting throughout the city would converge in a nearby plaza for rallies, and the children in Candice's classroom saw protesters walking by for many days. Some families participated in the protests and rallies. Candice wanted to serve as a resource for families as they talked to their children about why the protests were happening. She also wanted to address the issue in her classroom. Candice brought to bear her many years of working with three- and four-year-olds when finding ways to talk about things in the adult world in a way that was appropriate and accessible for young children. When discussing the protests with her students, Candice explained the situation this way:

> I said, "Some things have been happening over some time where people are not being treated fairly. So, somebody who does something wrong—if two people did the same wrong thing, they should have the same punishment." So I said—I didn't use our classroom—but I said, "Like at home, if you did something that your parents didn't like, what happens?" And they said, "Oh, I get a time out." And I said, "Well what if you get a time out and your brother did the same thing and he got to get ice cream?" And they were like, "No way! That's so unfair." And I said, "Well sometimes things like that happen, but in the grown-up world." So I said, "People are protesting because they noticed that sometimes people with brown skin don't get the same treatment if they got into trouble, or even if they just wanted to go someplace."

Note that in talking to her students about the reason people were protesting, Candice did not introduce any traumatizing information, but presented the issue in terms that students could understand and relate to.

Fostering children's capacity for empathy involves giving them opportunities for perspective taking, for putting themselves in the shoes of another person, even if they have not experienced what that person has experienced. Candice started by asking all of the children to consider how it would feel for them to see punishment and privilege doled out inequitably and arbitrarily. This taps young children's innate orientation toward fairness. Once their investment in the issue of inequity was engaged, Candice explained that the protests were not just about inequitable treatment applied randomly, but in response to an observed pattern tied to race. Educators like Candice skillfully offer children opportunities to process difficult things in a culturally sustaining and developmentally appropriate way that helps them to make sense of what is happening in the world. Developing the skill to do this well is essential for all early childhood educators, as children bring their questions and concerns about the world into the classroom and educators must be prepared to respond.

Responding in the Moment

Precious, who identifies as African American and Native American, and Esperanza, who identifies as Mexican, teach three- and four-year-olds together at Family First Early Head Start. The majority of the students are African American, but the year I interviewed them, there was one White child in the classroom named Annabella. When I asked the teachers to recall a teachable moment related to race and racism, Precious offered the following story:

> [Annabella] said to one of the children, "Why are you so ugly? Your skin is dark. Why are you so ugly?" And, you know, I was so shocked I didn't know how to respond. . . . I didn't quite know how to respond at that time because I had never experienced a racist remark between two students. But I did address it. We did address it.

Precious and Esperanza addressed this incident in two ways. They began by speaking with the child who said the racist thing. Esperanza sat down with her and explained that what she had said was hurtful and that in their classroom they practice kindness toward their friends. After speaking with the child one-on-one, Precious and Esperanza developed a short unit of curriculum for the whole class. They read and discussed several books about how people have different colored skin, hair texture, and eye color, depending on where in the world their families come from. They talked with the children about how people are the same and how they are different. The teachers described the ways that they themselves were different from each other. "We talked about [Esperanza] coming from Mexico. We talked about me [Precious] being Native American. We talked about other children who come from Caribbean. We talked about Annabella's father coming from Italy." After guiding the class in describing the ways that they were different and the ways that they were similar, Precious posed the following question for discussion: "Should we be treated differently because of the color of our skin?" They then invited the children to reflect on their own experiences. Precious noted:

> I think we opened up the doors for children to have their critical thinking or their own opinions or their own knowledge on what racism is, without using the word *racism*. And I think that through experiences with their friends who look different from them, I think they're able to come up with their own analysis of if a person is good or a person is bad, based on the color of their skin. And I would think that the answer would be no. No. People are just different.

In working with Annabella and the whole class, Precious and Esperanza offered the children a counternarrative to the racial bias that young children begin to absorb as a function of living in a racist society. Esperanza and Precious capitalized on a teachable moment to develop curriculum that offered an opportunity for growth for the whole community. It is clear that when racism emerges in our classrooms we must find ways to address it. However, the educators did not describe how they cared for the child to whom Annabella had said racist things in the first place.

Lara, who identifies as White and Italian American, is a prekindergarten teacher at the Green Public School. She described how over time she has grown and changed in her understanding of how to address incidents of racism in the classroom. In all cases when harm is inflicted in our classrooms, our first inclination is usually to make sure that the child whose behavior was hurtful understands what they did was wrong. In turning our attention to the child who does harm, however, we might unintentionally be neglecting the child who has been harmed. Lara has learned that especially in incidents of racism, it is essential she first turn her attention to the child who has been the subject of the hurtful comment or behavior. Recalling an incident where one child told a Black girl in her classroom that she "smelled like poop because she was brown," Lara explained her response:

> I think everyone when you hear something like that, it's so stark you think, "I have to address the person that said it. That's so rude and hurtful and it's unacceptable and it

can't be said." You know? It's the kind of thing that you feel you have to jump on. But what I'm learning is that it's really important to address the kid who's getting hurt immediately. Because that is the sort of thing that is unacceptable even if it seems harmless, and is not a thing that the other kid who's doing the harm is understanding.

That's the kind of thing that, when you reflect with grown-ups on their earliest racism experiences, that's the kind of stuff they remember. You know? Like, "This was said, and it wasn't treated like a big deal. And I was really upset about it and it happened in pre-K." It's different to be someone who's learning about racism than to be someone who experiences racism. And it's a privilege to be someone who's just learning about it.

As time goes on, I'm realizing it's really more important to address the person who is getting hurt first to show that you care and know that it's unacceptable. And then talk to the person that said the thing that was hurtful. . . . That's the kind of thing that when you're really young and you have those kind of experiences and you're the one experiencing the racism, that's the kind of stuff that really stays with you and shapes your experience of school. So I do think there's a matter of addressing it then and sort of teaching to it after.

Again, while many teachers might first address the person who has done the harm, Lara's orientation toward the recipient of the harm comes from the sensitivity she has gained through being part of conversations with other adults about their experiences of race and racism. In anti-racism training, it is common for participants to recall and share their earliest memories of race. As a White person socialized to believe in a color-evasive (Jones 2025) world, I was never aware of how early my friends of color experienced racism firsthand, and it was especially important for me to learn this as an educator. As a White educator who has participated in professional development focused on racial awareness, Lara likely learned from hearing the stories of friends and colleagues of the global majority how the racism they experienced as a child went unaddressed by the adults in their lives. This perspective has given Lara an awareness that when incidents like this occur in her classroom, the most urgent need is to attend to the child who has been the subject of racism. Some teachers may not take the time to do this, perhaps because their energy turns toward addressing the child who did the racist behavior or because they do not want to draw attention to the racism. As Lara reminds us, the child who has done the racist behavior needs to learn why their behavior is unacceptable, but their learning can wait a moment while the child who has been harmed receives care and repair.

Colette, Hannah, and Jordana are a team of teachers working with three- and four-year-olds at the Grasshopper Montessori Private Preschool. Colette identifies as Grenadian, or Black and Caribbean. Hannah identifies as White and as from New England. Jordana identifies as Brazilian, White, and Latino. I had the pleasure to interview this teaching team as a group in 2019, two years before I met most of the other teachers, as they agreed to help me pilot the interview questions as I was developing this project. This timing is important to note, as I know many teachers changed their approach to teaching about race and racism in their classrooms after the racial reckoning we experienced in the summer of 2020.

As I described in the chapter on teaching about race, Colette, Hannah, and Jordana developed curriculum that provided children with an opportunity to learn about different cultures and cultural traditions, but as Jordana shared, "We never tackled race actively and directly." In the previous chapter, Hannah shared the tension she feels teaching about cultures different from her own when doing this work as a White teacher. Additionally, like many private schools, Grasshopper Montessori serves predominantly White families. When I interviewed the team in 2019, they shared that they did not do any teaching to specifically address the topic of racism. However, they described several times when they addressed racism when it was visible in their classroom. When I asked if there had been any teachable moments when they had to respond to children's observations or questions about race, Hannah shared the following story:

> There was one time—I didn't witness it directly, but it happened in our classroom. It was three years ago. One of our young children, a White child, said something about one teacher being better than the other teacher because this teacher had lighter skin. Like, literally, these are words

coming out of this child's mouth. And it was startling, because we knew the parents, and I couldn't possibly imagine that this message is something that these parents have ever provided. But it speaks into that idea if children aren't explicitly taught before the age of eight that we're all freakin' fantastic, then it solidifies that what's "other"—what was darker than this child—was not as good.

Earlier in the interview, Hannah had shared that reading the book *Nurture Shock* by Po Bronson had been transformative in informing her thinking about how to talk about race with her own children. The book provided evidence that young children are aware of race and absorb racism when they are very young, and this solidified Hannah's commitment as a White parent to talk with her White children about race. Nonetheless, she did not teach about racism proactively with her teaching team, though she and the team were highly attuned to responding to incidents of racism in their classroom.

While the incident above had occurred in the classroom several years prior, it prompted Jordana to share a story from another classroom that had just occurred the previous week. As part of her Montessori credentialing, Jordana had participated in workshops about teaching about race and racism. The school administrators had asked her to lead in-house workshops at Grasshopper to share what she was learning with the rest of the school staff. Just before our interview, Jordana had led a session for colleagues introducing them to a variety of children's books that talk about race. She shared that during the session, one of the other teachers had told them that in her class, "There was a situation in which a White child looked at a dark-skinned child and told him he was a monkey." Jordana clarified that this comment did not come when the children were engaged in dramatic play or pretending to be animals. She also shared that the teacher confessed that she did not know how to respond in the moment. This story makes it clear that we need to do more to prepare teachers for how to respond to incidents of racism in the early childhood classroom, and again, that teachers should consider developing curriculum that addresses race and racism proactively, so that it is not always being introduced in a moment of crisis.

Finally, Colette offered a story from their classroom that had taken place several years before that still lingered in her consciousness. She recalled:

> Kids pick up on things and they see. There was this one kid that noticed that he was the only Black child that was in the room.... And there were kids who I heard before say, "Oh, this brown boy right there." So, they do see those things. And that child, they felt a way because they pointed out that they were the only brown child in the class....
> [A child] came to me and he said, "This brown-skinned boy right here." I don't know if he wanted something that the other child had. But, I'm like, "He has a name. You can call him by his name."

As the only other person in the room with brown skin, Colette brought a thoughtful sensitivity to the experience of a Black child being identified in a way that drew attention to their difference in a predominantly White environment. Colette's assertion that all children should be called by their name demonstrates her attunement to making sure that each child is known fully and treated with dignity. These stories also serve as a reminder that we need to be prepared to lay the foundation proactively for children to be able to talk about race and difference.

Samara, who identifies as Middle Eastern, works as an assistant teacher in a public school that serves predominantly African American children and families. Though she is not responsible for developing curriculum herself, she expressed great respect for Ms. James, one of the teachers in her classroom, who responded when anti-Asian bias emerged during the COVID-19 pandemic. New York City schools have the day off for Lunar New Year, and when the teacher explained the meaning of the holiday, children responded by saying, " 'Oh, we don't like Chinese.... They gave us COVID.' " Using the school's process of restorative circles, Ms. James learned that many of the children were processing various forms of trauma related to the pandemic. Unearthing the fear that undergirded the students' bias created an opportunity. She explained to the children that the messages they had been receiving from adults and the media that they should blame people from China for the pandemic were both false and harmful because they stoked bias and hate. Samara recalled, "[Ms. James] had to explain to them that it's not fair for any type of people to be hurt or attacked for how they look. She told them, 'It doesn't matter how you look. We're all humans.' " Additionally, Ms. James developed a curriculum that explained the meaning of Lunar New Year and how it is celebrated. Samara observed that the students were highly engaged in this unit. Though their initial reaction was to resist learning about the holiday, Samara shared, "At the end of the lesson they started looking for what the year was for. Like there's the Year of the Dog, the Year of the Rabbit. So they started looking at their years, what year they were born and what that was. So I thought that was [a] great way for them to connect." Samara appreciated the way that Ms. James offered the children an opportunity to learn about and appreciate Asian culture and heritage. Connecting with and valuing the culture of people different from oneself can help a child resist bias when they hear it expressed by the grown-ups in their world.

Impact on Children

In this chapter we have explored ways that teachers have developed planned curriculum to teach about racism, and also how they responded to racist incidents in their classrooms. In the next chapter, we will explore some more examples of this work by visiting five classrooms in which teaching about race and racism is deeply integrated throughout the curriculum throughout the year. To conclude this chapter, I will share some of the teachers' reflections on the effect this work has had on students and on themselves as teachers. Lola, a prekindergarten teacher at the Kellman Public School, shared observations of her own classroom:

> There have been a lot of moments where kids have gotten emotional. Where kids have said things that have made me realize how impactful the lesson may be for them. . . . But I can say I've never walked away and said, "Oh, I shouldn't have done that" or "I shouldn't have taught that" or "That was too much." I've always felt like I've given them enough, but I've never given them too much. I've always given them what they can handle. And it's to the benefit. I think it makes them wiser, it makes them more sympathetic. It makes them more empathetic, more understanding.

Lara, a prekindergarten teacher at the Green Public School, explained that she feels it is her responsibility as a teacher of young children to acknowledge that racism exists in the world and to make her classroom a space where children can process their thoughts and feelings about this troubling reality that they can see with their own eyes. She explained:

> I think there's a ton of things that people shield children from that I don't think they need to be shielded from. They just need to be explained in a concise, simple—not simplified, but simple—way for them to understand. Because kids can really understand a lot, and we shouldn't underestimate their ability to digest what's going on. Because chances are they're digesting what's going on. But, if they don't have guidance, they're the ones filling in information in their heads. . . . Or they're creating a story that isn't true out of the pieces that they're putting together, which is where racism starts to build in young children. Because if it's not being talked about, they're filling in blanks on their own.

Children's curiosity means they are always observing and absorbing everything they see, hear, and touch. They use this information to identify patterns and to draw conclusions about how the world works. As Lara reminds us, we need to make sure children have access to information that helps them to draw conclusions that are not grounded in bias and hate. For example, if on the walk to school a child passes people who are unhoused, and notices that many of them are Black, they might conclude that "Dark-skinned people are not good at finding homes." If a child hears adults in their life describe a place where people of the global majority live as a "bad" neighborhood, they will learn racial bias against people with those racial identities, including when those people look like them. And if children of all races observe that when schools sort children into the category of "gifted and talented," most of the children in those classrooms have lighter skin, they might conclude that only children with lighter skin have gifts and talents. Internalizing these conclusions is harmful for children of all races. If in our classrooms we recognize that racial bias has contributed to creating an unjust world, we can offer children tools to make sense of what they observe in ways that do not allow racism to fill the vacuum. In this way, children can join us in disrupting racism and in making the world a more just place for all of us.

CHAPTER 4

How We Create Anti-Racist Classrooms

Once I started working and being around a more diverse population of people, I got to see for myself that everybody is not the way they described one whole population to be. . . . It made my journey into education that much more significant to me. Because I say, "Here I am, I have these children in my hands. I have to implement tolerance and peace, and how to take care of the Earth, and all these philosophies, in these children who I have the power to change." . . . It really made me want to eliminate racism at the core, at the root, with these young children from all walks of life, from all diverse communities, with the power that I had as their teacher.

—Audre, interview transcript

A number of the educators I interviewed demonstrated a very sophisticated understanding of how to integrate teaching and learning about race and racism into their curriculum in ways that are culturally sustaining and developmentally appropriate. In the previous chapters I offered brief descriptions of the ways that many of the educators I interviewed address the topics of race and racism in their teaching. In what follows I will describe the work of several educators caring for young children at different ages and stages of development who demonstrate a deep and sustained commitment to incorporating anti-racist curriculum and pedagogy throughout their teaching practice. To demonstrate that early childhood educators can address these issues thoughtfully at all ages, I will offer portraits of five classrooms serving children from ages three to eight years old. Additionally, in each of the interviews, I asked teachers to share their reflections on their own racial identity development. Our own life experiences shape the lenses through which we view our work in the world, so the narratives that follow will include more information about the teachers and their identities as context.

Sapphire and Eliza's Three-Year-Old Classroom

> *I feel like the kinds of things that were talked about in my family were . . . anti-Semitism and things that happened to Jewish people, and . . . I don't really recall a lot of conversations about race when I was growing up.*
>
> —Eliza, interview transcript

> *I grew up in Jamaica. . . . I did not grow up seeing much White people except for in the tourist area. Half of my family is Black. Half of my family identifies as Indian. I grew up in two different parts of the world. My Black side of the family was very poor and my Indian side of the family was middle to upper class.*
>
> —Sapphire, interview transcript

Sapphire, who identifies as Black, and Eliza, who identifies as White, teach together in a three-year-old classroom at the Emilia Private School. I interviewed Sapphire and Eliza together as a teaching team. The school uses the Reggio Emilia approach, and the teachers are deeply invested in supporting the children's social and emotional growth. Eliza explained the school's predominantly White racial makeup as follows: "The nature of a private school means that our students pay tuition, which as you know has a certain impact on the kinds of families that have access to our school." The persistence of the racial wealth gap in the United States explains why many private schools, even those that prioritize racial diversity in admissions, are most often predominantly White spaces.

Sapphire grew up in Jamaica and came to New York when she was eighteen years old. Sapphire explained that growing up in Jamaica, "I didn't experience racism." That changed when she came to the United States. Even in Jamaica, however, as the daughter of a light-skinned Indian Jamaican father and a dark-skinned Afro-Caribbean mother, she was aware of one of the symptoms of white supremacy, the colorism that gets internalized in communities of color. She recalled:

> I can remember a lot of comments regarding colorism in my family. My Indian side of the family, they were all very light skinned, could pass as White. And there was always some conflict with my dad being with someone outside of his race. So I was very aware of that as a kid. I knew that I didn't look like my cousins. We all had different hair and different skin color. It was very obvious. They didn't talk about it in front of me, but I knew that they talked about it. And my mom was very aware of it, and she would say things to me when I was with her. But when I was with my Indian side of the family, it was never said in front of me but I was aware of it.

Arriving in the United States, Sapphire became much more aware of race, particularly after starting her job at the Emilia School, where both the families and the staff are mostly White. She explained that she became "very much aware of race. Not because of the people here—everyone here is just amazing and incredible—but just because of how everyone was tiptoeing around the topic of race here. Just not really saying anything about it." It felt disorienting for Sapphire to enter a predominantly White space where the fact of race seemed to go unacknowledged. Sapphire explained that in adulthood, in the United States, in a school that is predominantly White, race is something she thinks about all the time:

> Sometimes it feels like it's my whole life. But there have been some moments this year where . . . it hasn't felt like that. It hasn't felt like I'm constantly talking about my identity and my race and other people, or just race in general. It takes up a lot of space in your life. I find myself talking about the [ways we are addressing race] here to my friends outside of the school. I'm just constantly talking about it. But, I don't know, it's just a big part of me this year. And it's been a big part of me for the past two years, I would say. But I definitely think that it's something

that I can't push to the side at all. And that it will be a part of me
for a very long time. Because it feels very important to me.

Sapphire's reflections on her experience of race reminded me of something I heard emphasized by Courtney Martin, who writes and speaks about race in education. Martin asserts that we need to be able to talk explicitly about race, especially in predominantly White spaces, because when whiteness is centered, it becomes simultaneously dominant but also invisible (Lefkowits 2021). When the fact of whiteness and racial privilege are unacknowledged, it can be disorienting, like a form of gaslighting, especially for people who are well aware of the role that race and racism play in our lives.

Eliza identifies as White and Jewish and was raised in a predominantly White suburb in New Jersey. She recalled that her awareness of issues of bias came primarily through her family's discussions of "anti-Semitism and things that happened to Jewish people. I don't really recall a lot of conversations about race when I was growing up." Like several of the other White teachers I interviewed, Eliza's racial awareness began to develop much more deeply when she began working in education. Eliza majored in Jewish studies for her undergraduate degree and later completed her master's at Bank Street College of Education, where she also worked in the school that was housed there. As a teacher at Bank Street, she participated in a professional development workshop offered by the organization Undoing Racism. Describing the impact this work had on her, Eliza explained:

> That was the first time that I realized the weight of race and racism in this country and in this city. And since then I've remained in private schools, all of whom have had a commitment in some regard to doing this kind of work; it definitely changed my understanding and experiences with racism and whiteness.

During their years of working as a teaching team, Sapphire and Eliza—supported by their colleagues at the Emilia School—have transformed how they teach and learn about race and racism with their classroom of three-year-olds.

Eliza is the lead teacher and is clearly a highly skilled educator. Though she has many more credits of education coursework and credentialing than Sapphire, as they described teaching and developing curriculum together, it was clear that Eliza had grown in her teaching through conversations with Sapphire and other school staff about how race comes to play in their classroom. It was a testament to the strength of their relationship as a teaching team, as well as the mentoring and support they received from other school staff, that Sapphire and Eliza were able to discuss issues of race and racism in their teaching with candor and vulnerability.

I interviewed the teachers in the spring of 2021 and asked them to describe how they teach and learn about race and racism in their classroom. Sapphire explained, "This year in particular, the main difference was that we just did it instead of waiting for it to come up." I asked the teachers to clarify how they came up with this proactive approach, and if it was in any way connected to the racial justice uprisings of the previous year. They explained that, in fact, they had already begun planning to be more proactive about teaching about race and racism before the summer of 2020. Sapphire recounted that the impetus for this change had come in part because of an incident two years prior, during her first year as a substitute teacher in Eliza's classroom. She recalled,

> My first year at Emilia was in Eliza's class. . . . And I was in the classroom and a kid said something about brown skin being dirtier. And I was actually very offended by it. I was lucky enough that the other teacher did a great job at handling it. . . . I had strong feelings about it. And at that time I didn't know how to handle it . . . but after that I remember having a conversation, following up with Eliza and the other teacher and also Sonia [the early childhood program director]. And through that conversation, that's when I think, Eliza, you started in your classroom reading books and going through this process that we're going through right now. But that happened late in the year. . . . I feel like where we are right now, they could not have done any of those things that year. So then after that incident happened there was this urgency to start talking about this with children, with the twos and threes.

Sapphire further clarified that the child's comment about dark skin being dirty was directed at her, the only person with brown skin in the classroom, and shared her strong feelings about this incident. Feeling both understandably emotional and also less experienced as a teacher, Sapphire felt unprepared to respond in the moment, and she acknowledged her appreciation that Andrew, the other teacher present at the time of this incident, addressed the issue appropriately. Yet neither Eliza nor Andrew, both White teachers, had planned to proactively offer the children opportunities to talk about and learn about race as part of their planned curriculum.

Reflecting on this incident now, Sapphire observed that it offered a turning point for the school staff in thinking about how they teach about race and racism with young children. She recalled:

> I feel like the problem was that people were waiting until children brought this up. And the better thing that we could do was just start. Because if they bring it up in March, there's not enough time to talk about it. There's not enough time to go through the process of what we're doing right now, like starting small and getting to the bigger things. So that was my first experience at the Emilia School. And it's been three years, and the whole process has just been incredible, how everyone has taken on this work. It's in every classroom. And ... some parents are having a hard time with it, but all teachers and everyone at Emilia has stayed committed to doing the work and it's incredible. I'm pleasantly surprised by the effort that everyone has put in this year and it brings me great joy. That they're doing the work.

Sapphire is generous in her appreciation of the ways that the Emilia staff have come together to change the ways that they teach about race and racism with young children. Yet it is clear that her presence as the only Black teacher at the time, and her courage in sharing her discomfort, provided the catalyst for this change.

This change in approach to teaching and learning with young children about race and racism manifested in the thoughtfully designed curriculum and approach to teaching that Sapphire and Eliza implemented in their classroom. Using what they know about the development of two- and three-year-olds, the teachers focused on offering the children opportunities to observe and describe differences in a way that would strengthen their capacity to talk about race. As the school follows the Reggio Emilia philosophy, the teachers invest a great deal of energy in preparing the environment of the classroom and in offering materials that provoke the children's growth and learning. They explained that they began the year by filling the shelves with materials that were all different shades of brown. Eliza described their process:

> We've done that for a couple of years now as a beginning-of-the-year practice, and then bringing other colors in slowly after they've developed a language around working with the shades of brown. Because then they have to use other language. You can't just say, "Pass me the yellow." You have to say, like, "Can you pass me that tannish brown one? Oh, not that one, the one that's a little darker than that." You know, and they just like start making up ways to talk about it. I mean, I could show you our tray . . . [*displays tray of ten very lovely oil pastels in all shades of brown*]—like, when this is what you have, and you need someone to pass you the brown, well, "Which brown?" So it sparks interesting—kids are so creative and flexible in the way that they think. It's just interesting to figure it all out.

Eliza continued, explaining the purpose of the lesson:

> [The aim was to have students practice] colloquially discussing shades of brown in relation to objects as well as skin. And building an appreciation for the shades of brown in the world. And then as we were talking about what you call "the color of your skin," we also touched on other aspects of your identity . . . and giving kids ownership over the words that they like to use to describe themselves and the people in their families.

This intentional approach to the provisioning of classroom materials laid the foundation for teachers to begin to talk with children about racial differences. As described in chapter 2, when the teachers at the Emilia School cannot find an existing children's book that offers language to discuss a particular issue, they create one themselves. Sapphire recounted that these conversations gave these very young children the skills that most adults, due to a combination of fear and lack of practice, have difficulty with observing and describing racial differences in a way that makes others feel visible and affirmed. Sapphire observed the value in these learning experiences:

> [We were] giving them language to ask other people [about the color of their skin]. And ever since we've done that, I've had many instances where one of my kids, if I see her, she would just randomly ask me, "Uh, Sapphire, what do you call your skin again?" So, I mean, they're really internalizing all of it and practicing it.

Eliza observed the impact that this approach to curriculum and pedagogy had on the children's social and emotional development:

> [Through the curriculum, we were] developing [children's] muscle around the empathy aspect of it. So instead of just saying, "Oh, you have a beard"—instead of making observations—checking in with someone before defining them in some way. And I think because we do that so often, they've internalized why it feels good to them. . . . We would never define them. Because we're constantly checking in or helping children check in with each other, they know that it feels good to be able to name it yourself as opposed to being named.

Sapphire and Eliza knew that spending many weeks with this curriculum would offer a necessary foundation for introducing the topic of racism. Once they felt the children had developed fluency in talking about race, they found ways to talk with the children about the fact that adults use racial differences as a reason to treat people unfairly. After four months of infusing the curriculum with opportunities to teach and learn about race, the teachers used the occasion of Martin Luther King Jr. Day to discuss the impact of racism in history and today. Once again, they created their own book for the children, making sure to connect the story of King's life and the civil rights movement to struggles for justice at the present moment. Eliza explained the purpose of the book:

> [We wanted to] tell the story about how Martin Luther King believed in using his words to advocate for things being fair for all people. And at the end, instead of painting a rosy picture, saying Martin Luther King is one person who worked really hard to change some of these unfair laws and rules, and people still work really hard today to make sure that people are treated fairly.

Sapphire and Eliza have been thoughtful about how and when to introduce particular language and concepts to the children. They shared that many of the children in their classroom are aware of the contemporary movement for racial justice. When the class sees Black Lives Matter signs on neighborhood walks, the children have shared that they and their families have attended marches where these signs are used. Our interview took place in mid-March, two months after the teachers began introducing lessons about racism, but Eliza shared, "We have not used the word *racism* with our group yet—explicitly that word—because developmentally, we just haven't gotten there yet. I think they could probably handle it, but usually we refer to it as a law, or a set of laws, of beliefs that are unfair." Sapphire concurred: "This doesn't feel like the right time yet." But the teachers continued to observe and be responsive to when the children would be ready for new information.

Sapphire and Eliza continued throughout that school year to offer models of people of the global majority who are living and thriving today. The inauguration of President Joe Biden and Vice President Kamala Harris offered them multiple opportunities to celebrate the contributions of people of the global majority. Eliza described their process:

> We kept our ear open to current events and thought carefully about when and what felt appropriate to share with them. Did we tell them the story of George Floyd? No. But Amanda Gorman's poem from Joe Biden's inauguration, we looked at and listened to many times. We learned about who she is and

why she had the opportunity to speak. Actually that whole inauguration was something that they were really interested in, so we talked about that particular event a lot, and Kamala Harris being the first Black female in the White House. So, appreciating that some events in the world might be a lot for kids who are three and four years old to grapple with, but finding ways for them to connect and find meaning.

I asked all of the teachers I interviewed to share with me any conversations they have had with their students' families and with their colleagues about this work. In most of their reported conversations with families, parents asked teachers for suggestions about how to respond when children make observations about race. However, Sapphire and Eliza did hear from one family who criticized the content of the curriculum. Eliza described the interaction:

> [The parent said,] "My child is separating the light-colored peg people from the dark-colored peg people, and she never would have done that if you hadn't introduced it. She never would have known that that was something to do." . . . So we gave them a pretty lengthy description about why we made the choices we made and why we feel like it's important, and the different developmental elements that we have considered in talking about all of this. They didn't push much further.

Many teachers who incorporate explicit conversations about race and racial difference into their curriculum face resistance from families. Sapphire and Eliza found ways to explain their curricular choices. They were also fortified in their commitment to continue teaching this content when they observed that the students in their classroom were becoming knowledgeable about race at such a young age. As Eliza shared with Sapphire's agreement, "I actually think it's kind of ironic that I think the children in this class are more well versed in speaking about this topic than I think most of the other people in my life. Like in my family."

When families object to curriculum that addresses race and racism, educators must be able to articulate how their curriculum is grounded in developmentally appropriate and culturally sustaining practice. Both educators expressed appreciation for the support they received from Sonia, the director of the early childhood program at Emilia School, who is White, and for the conversations she facilitated with the early childhood teaching staff about issues of race and racism inside their classrooms and in the outside world. The early childhood teaching team held regularly scheduled times for reflective conversations, and it was at one of these meetings that Sapphire was able to process concerns arising for her out of dramatic play in the classroom. At the meeting, Sonia noticed that Sapphire had been unusually quiet as Eliza described police–bad guy play that they had observed. Sonia invited Sapphire to share any observations she had, and Sapphire responded:

> [I told Sonia:] "Actually, I'm still processing all of this. I don't feel very good about it. . . . I'm still processing my feelings about police. I haven't thought about it in a long time, and this game brought up those feelings for me. And I need a moment to process before I can even think about what to do next." . . . And then I think two days after, one of the kids asked if I could be the bad guy in the game. And I said, "Okay, sure, I'll play the game." And the game actually turned out to be really fun. . . . But I did have those feelings when the game just started. Very strong feelings of not wanting to play. . . . But then when I did join the game it was actually very light and very simple and very fun.

One thing that helped Sapphire to process her reaction to police–bad guy play was that her concerns and feelings were taken seriously by her colleagues. Eliza joined with Sapphire in paying attention to the implications of the game and stood ready to respond to any teachable moments that arose. They recounted:

> ELIZA:
>
> We tried to dig into what they knew or didn't know about police. . . . It turns out they know very little. We did talk together professionally about what are our responsibilities

in terms of helping them understand police and some of the problematic pieces of police in America. . . . But it didn't come to that because when you actually played the game it was so juvenile, the game itself. It's about chase and be chased. . . . It's all the things that three- and four-year-olds work on and are interested in. But it's not really about police and policing and the police system. *[Sapphire nods.]* They really were actually pretty unable to articulate anything a police officer does or anything that might land a person in jail. . . . When we tried to dig, we basically found out that they're still playing this through right now, and maybe if it consistently remains a theme maybe we can open their eyes to a couple of pieces. But for now it was really more about learning to play, not about the police system in America.

SAPPHIRE:

It's a little tricky to know when to dive deeper into these things. And this was one of the moments where we didn't need to.

ELIZA:

We definitely considered it.

SAPPHIRE:

We did.

Planning to teach about race and racism is complex and important work. It takes great skill for all educators to develop the nuanced perspective necessary to respond in the moment. For Sapphire and Eliza, it was critically important that they had already established a mutually respectful and trusting relationship so they could process the choices they were faced with in their teaching. They were supported in this work in the shared space created by Sonia, the early childhood program director, for the early childhood team to grow and learn together. The team participated in multiple professional development workshops about race and racism. During the summer, each teacher read a book on the topic and brought back what they had learned. Sapphire and Eliza also expressed appreciation for school administrators who facilitated conversations with families about these issues. Sapphire reflected: "It's very impactful to have the teacher and leadership and parents all in one conversation."

While it is possible for educators to do this work on their own, Sapphire and Eliza's thoughtful and intentional work was made possible through their collaboration and the support they drew from many directions. According to some measures, Sapphire was one of the least experienced and least credentialed teachers on the staff, but her willingness to raise important questions and concerns and the openness of her White colleagues to respond to them enabled a process that allowed them to grow collectively in their capacity to teach and learn with young children.

Jasmine's Four-Year-Old Classroom

> *At the time, I didn't realize what I was feeling. I was feeling this ickiness of racism. . . . And it was the first time I can remember feeling difference. Like an us-and-them kind of situation.*
>
> —Jasmine, interview transcript

Jasmine is a prekindergarten teacher at the Green Public School, a small, progressive public elementary school. Historically, the Green School has sought to enroll a racially and economically diverse population of students. While the school still serves a multiracial community, all three of the Green School teachers I interviewed noted a widening in the range of families' socioeconomic status over the past few years due to gentrification in the neighborhood, which has many public housing developments as well as increasingly expensive privately owned apartments. Jasmine also noted that the school serves a large number of LGBTQ+ families. The school staff is racially diverse, though most staff who are people of the global majority serve as assistant teachers or school aides. Jasmine is one of only a few lead teachers who is a person of the global majority.

Jasmine, who identifies as West Indian, grew up in the Bronx in what she described as a "predominantly Black and Brown community with all of my friends either being Black or Dominican or Puerto Rican." Though Jasmine was only one of two Indo Caribbean (Hindu and Guyanese) students at her school, she felt a strong sense of solidarity and belonging throughout her elementary school years. Starting middle school, Jasmine was offered the opportunity to attend a magnet school for students who had demonstrated high academic performance in elementary school that was located in another neighborhood in the Bronx. Her middle school served mostly Black and Latino students, but was located in the same building as a predominantly White public school. Jasmine was immediately struck by two things: First, that the neighborhood around their school was unlike any other she had ever seen in the Bronx, with "sprawling green grass and trees and huge houses." *Second*, it was made abundantly clear that she and her classmates were not welcome in other parts of the school building or in the neighborhood. She recalled being prohibited from going on other floors in the school building that housed the predominantly White school. Additionally, each day when dismissed from school, Jasmine and her classmates were greeted by New York City police officers who were stationed to prevent the students from walking in front of the synagogue across the street. Jasmine still vividly remembered getting lost while taking the bus to the new neighborhood on the first day of school. As a vulnerable, distraught twelve-year-old, she asked other passengers if she could use their mobile phone to call for directions, and they refused. She quickly learned how she was being viewed:

> I was leaving my neighborhood and going to a predominantly White neighborhood. It was my first day of using public transportation. I was sobbing and nobody on the bus would help me. No one wanted me to use their phone. I had to promise people that I wouldn't steal their phone, because I realized that that's the thing that they thought I was going to do.

Memories like this have sealed Jasmine's commitment to making sure that every child and family in her classroom feels welcomed and affirmed, and that her work as a teacher be part of the project of dismantling racism.

Like many of the teachers I spoke with, Jasmine designs curriculum that explores race through children's literature, self-portraits, and a study of different cultures. Additionally, Jasmine knows that good early childhood curriculum follows children's curiosity and interests, and she described the ways that she is responsive to ideas that emerge from in-class discussions. On the topic of race in particular, Jasmine explained:

> I think a lot of it is just allowing conversation to happen. I feel like there can be conversations that feel too heavy to handle. And some people can think, "Oh, that's a loaded topic to talk about with a small child." But I feel like welcoming all of those conversations of when kids notice that they're different from each other.

While many teachers who lack fluency in talking about race may shy away from the observations and questions that children raise, Jasmine draws on her own life experiences, which strengthen her commitment to following her students in their exploration of identity.

In addition to providing her students with opportunities to learn about race and to celebrate their identities, Jasmine incorporates opportunities to learn about racism and other forms of bias, as well as movements to bring about equity and justice. Like most young children, the four- and five-year-olds in Jasmine's class are very attuned to issues to fairness, and Jasmine's curriculum offers them opportunities to consider how they can stand up for themselves and for others. Jasmine recalled a time when the class was reading a book about Ruth Bader Ginsburg. One of the Jewish children in her class, whose mother is from Israel, noticed a sign in a restaurant in the illustration of the book that said, "No Blacks. No Jews. No dogs." The child responded strongly, shouting,

> "What does that mean?!?" And he was like, "But I'm Jewish." And I was like, "I know. Right? How unfriendly is this sign? No Black people, no Jewish people, and no dogs. Comparing people to animals. How unfriendly. Let's talk about how you feel." And he was like, "No." And he turned around and he wouldn't talk to us. And so I stopped reading the book and I said, "I noticed you're having some really big feelings and if you don't want to talk about them, that's fine. But if you do want to talk about them right now, we don't have to keep on reading the book, we can stop and talk about it." And we did.

> We stopped and talked about how words can make people feel and how exclusion can make people feel. And it was this really beautiful conversation.

In a follow-up conversation with the child's mother, Jasmine learned the mother was deeply grateful that her child had the opportunity to process learning about this history in the safe space of Jasmine's classroom. The mother explained that as a child in Israel she had learned about the Holocaust as soon as she started school and had been preparing to have to share this painful history with her child. She was appreciative that her child had already found the opportunity to process a piece of this history with his peers and teacher. Jasmine continued to build on the conversation by exploring more books about bias and about fights for racial justice, civil rights, and LGBTQ+ rights. Jasmine's intentional approach to designing curriculum allowed the class to explore "that idea that injustice against one is injustice against all."

In addition to her planned and emergent curriculum, Jasmine has not shied away from addressing internalized and interpersonal racism when it occurs in her classroom. She recalled one year when all of the White girls in her class formed a very tight clique and refused to play with any of the girls of the global majority. Additionally, there was an incident in which one of the White girls refused to hold the hand of a Black child in the class, saying, "I don't want to hold his hand because his skin is dirty." Jasmine spoke directly with the child one-on-one, saying, "'Well, my skin is the same color as his skin, so do I have dirty skin as well?' And she didn't know what to say. And I was like, 'I'm not upset. I just want to understand what you're thinking about.'" Jasmine felt that it was important to speak directly to the child about the racial dynamics of the incident. She explained that her goal was not to have the child apologize per se, but to make sure the child understood the implications of her behavior.

> I feel like addressing her one-on-one helped not shame her. I think there's a lot of shame that comes with talking about it. Because they're just like, "Uh oh. I did something wrong, but I don't know what's the wrong thing that I did." And so, I try to keep like a very even voice so that they don't think that I'm upset. . . . It's not that I want you to apologize. I want you

to find a way to make this person feel better. I want you to
be accountable for your actions, right? And respond to that
accountability.

When issues of racism come up in our classrooms, many teachers are uncomfortable addressing the issue directly. We may offer children a generic statement: "That's not nice—say you're sorry." In doing this, we fail to be explicit about why the words and actions are harmful—how they are so hurtful because they involve racial bias and exclusion.

Jasmine addressed the dynamics of White girls and their exclusionary play through whole-class conversations during which she shared with the class her concerns about what she was observing. Her strategy in addressing this issue was informed by what she knows about child development and what she knew about the children in her class and what they would be able to hear. She explained:

> I name the thing. Because I think with small children, sometimes talking around the situation doesn't get anywhere. I said, "I noticed some friends aren't including friends with skin colors like mine or darker skin colors. And I'm wondering what's happening." That year I had this really together class who were able to talk about it: "Well, I like playing with people who look like me." So then we read books about school-aged children not being able to go to school with other kids and they were like, "Oh, that's so unfair!" And I said, "It feels like that's what's happening right now in our classroom." And they were like, "Well, we don't want to be like that." And I said, "You don't have to be like that. And I'm not telling you you're like that. But I'm telling you this is the feeling that I'm getting in class and it's not feeling good."

In addition to using children's literature as a way to initiate conversation about hard topics like exclusion, Jasmine also uses puppet shows. Because narratives in the books and puppet shows mirror the dynamics of the classroom through the perspective of other characters, Jasmine explains that "I feel like a lot of the time, really hard conversations are dealt with through animals, which in one way is nice because it takes away the blame and the shaming part." However, in class discussions that follow, Jasmine circles back to the connection that the stories have to what is happening in her classroom, because she wants the children to recognize that "these things aren't happening with animals, they're happening with people, people that you care about and you have feelings for, so let's address it that way."

Jasmine reports that families that include people of the global majority seek her out for support and resources related to the ways that their children are internalizing racism. (These conversations are documented in more detail in later chapters on teachers' work with families.) Jasmine brings to this work her perspective as an educator who is a person of the global majority, attuned to issues of race and racism with particular sensitivity and perspective. She takes the responsibility of nurturing young children's growth and learning very much to heart and sees it as an opportunity to make the world more fair and just for all of us. She explains:

> We have to do it. It's not something that can be brushed aside or thought of, like, "They're too young" or "They don't understand this." Because children see differences, and they notice them all the time. We want children to be the stewards of our world. They're going to grow up and they're going to be people in this world with one another, and I want them to also speak love and kindness and honesty into one another as they get older. Because I can't be with them all the time. I have to let these children go and be their own people.

Cleo's Five-Year-Old Classroom

> *My parents didn't talk about race that much either with us. We did have a housekeeper who was Black, in our family, and she still works for my family. She's worked with my mom— my mom thinks of her as her friend. But as more than just a friend; she's like this very important person to my mom. But I think that's one of my mom's main interactions with a person of color, with a Black person who's been her housekeeper for, like, forty years.*
>
> —Cleo, interview transcript

Cleo is a White kindergarten/first-grade teacher working at the Peabody Public School, which serves a majority of Black and Latine children. As a child, Cleo was raised in a suburb that she described as "very White" and "very affluent." She recalled having one Black friend when she was growing up, and one of her earliest memories of being aware of race was at a playdate at her friend's house. She recalled, "I remember once I went into the bathroom at her house and she was like, 'Oh, make sure to put the fan on in the bathroom.' And I was like, 'Oh, I wonder if Black families like to have the fan on in the bathroom.'" As Cleo's recollection illustrates, when we live in largely segregated environments, we can tend to make sense of racial identity by applying what we know about one person to an entire race. In this case, wondering if all Black families use a fan in the bathroom is innocuous enough. However, many of us who grow up in racially segregated spaces can attach ourselves to assumptions and racial stereotypes quickly. Additionally, Cleo shared that the woman who cleaned her family's house may have been the only Black person her mother felt she knew well. Many White people have limited contact with people of the global majority, and when this contact does occur it is often mediated by an unequal power dynamic which makes it unlikely that authentic, mutual relationships can develop.

Cleo reflected that her process of racial self-awareness did not begin until adulthood when she began working in education. Cleo works in a school where the staff have engaged together in work around race, and she has sought out workshops and other opportunities to grow in her capacity to do this work. Investing in anti-racist professional development helps Cleo feel better able to build the connections she needs to have with children and families in order to be successful in her teaching. While this growth in her racial awareness has supported her work as a teacher, she has also noticed that it has an impact on her relationships with some of her White friends. She reflected:

> I try to talk about race with my friends too. And I'll name whiteness or white privilege with them in conversations a lot. But I've begun to tell which friends have thought about whiteness and which friends haven't as much yet.... I still have so much to learn and work on. But because I realize

> I've thought a lot about whiteness at this point and race for school purposes, then when I have conversations with friends I realize . . . They won't see certain things around white supremacist thinking as an issue. Or they won't know when I say white supremacy I'm not talking about KKK, I'm talking about general white supremacy. And so it brings a little bit of distance. I feel a little separate from them now.

The Peabody Public School where Cleo teaches follows a progressive, child-centered philosophy of teaching and learning. Every day, children have the opportunity for "work time" on the play-based activity of their choice. The school serves primarily Black and Latine families and, as Cleo described, "the students that are Black, in terms of ethnicity, are some Caribbean or Dominican or Haitian families and then in terms of Latine background Puerto Rican, Mexico, and other places." Every year there are also two or three White or Asian students in Cleo's class. Cleo is very aware that, as a White teacher who has spent most of her life in predominantly White spaces, the responsibility is on her to learn how to be successful in working with children and families of color. (Details about Cleo's additional professional development experiences can be found in the upcoming chapter focusing on teacher education and professional development.) These experiences have raised Cleo's consciousness about her own racial identity as a White person as well as offering her pedagogical strategies for teaching and learning about race and racism with young children.

Cleo creates opportunities to learn about race and to affirm her students' racial identities through a variety of activities. The class spends a lot of time on a study of families, again focusing on what is similar and what is unique about each person's family. It is important to Cleo that these activities do not just focus on physical characteristics, but that they include recognizing children's and families' interests and cultural traditions. Cleo seeks out books that offer her class language to understand and talk about race. Cleo reads *All the Colors We Are: The Story of How We Get Our Skin Color* by Katie Kissinger, which offers her class an understanding of how melanin works and how our ancestry influences what shade of brown everyone's skin is. Karen Katz's book *The Colors of Us* supports Cleo's class as they mix paint to achieve their skin color for self-portraits and use more specific and complex vocabulary (golden brown or tawny beige, for example) to describe their skin. These resources have helped Cleo to spark lively conversations with the children in her class.

While Cleo uses book discussions and self-portraits to offer her students a more varied range of ways to describe their skin color, she also believes it is important to help them understand that race is a social construction that at the same time has real implications in the world. She shared insights she has taken from trainings offered by the Center for Racial Justice in Education:

> It's not just skin color. It's race and the idea of race. We have to talk about it, and it ends up being very real for kids. But it can be a little confusing for kids because there's people who have very, very light skin who identify as Black, people who have different shades of hair. It's very much not these neat categories. But obviously it affects our whole world, so we need to be able to talk about this idea of race in addition to skin color. It can't just be concretely, like, "Everyone's shades of brown." Because it's race also, which is this big idea that affects their lives.

Additionally, Cleo has learned from her trainings on racial injustice that it is especially important for her as a White teacher to name her whiteness in conversations with her class. She shares her insight:

> It's very important for them, the kids, to hear you say things like "White people like me." And to say that you're White. And not just be like, I'm a neutral body who's sitting and talking about race. . . . To say it and name it. Because otherwise it's like whiteness is neutral, whiteness is the standard, whiteness doesn't exist. It's people of color who must be named and talked about.

Cleo's explicit acknowledgment of her own White racial identity also provides a framework for her to talk about the responsibility White people have to address racism and dismantle the myth of white supremacy. She has appreciated the opportunity that books like *Our Skin: A First Conversation About Race* by Megan Madison and Jessica Ralli provide by explaining what racism and white supremacy are using language that children can understand. Cleo recalled a conversation that arose during a discussion of the book:

> One of my students was like, "Yeah, Black Lives Matter." And I was like, "Yeah, you know, White people like me have a lot of work to do to really help make sure that racism stops. Because we're the people who, you know, a long time ago, created this issue and it's still a problem today."

Cleo's class has also viewed a video created by PBS Kids featuring Amanda Gorman's poetry for children that addresses race and racism and offers children the opportunity to envision the role they can play in bringing about a more just world.

Despite the variety of ways that Cleo seeks to incorporate discussion of race and racism into the curriculum, she also needs to be prepared to respond when the racism that children have internalized arises in the classroom. She recalled a particularly challenging and troubling incident that occurred in class when she was reading Derrick Barnes's book *I Am Every Good Thing*. The book is narrated by a young Black boy who shares all of the things that make him proud of himself. Books like this are critically important to include in classroom libraries and discussions, as they function to counteract the numerous messages of anti-Blackness that children of all races absorb in the world. During the read-aloud, Cleo used strategies to engage young children's literacy development. She showed the class the cover of the book and asked them to share their thoughts, feelings, and predictions on what the book was about. Cleo described what followed:

> When we looked at the front of the book—It's a picture of the boy on the front, he's crossing his arms and he's kind of [*Cleo mimics an expression of confidence*] self-assured, from what I could tell. And the background of the book is red. And one of my students who was Black raised his hand and said, "He looks confident." And one of my White students—one of my two White students, a girl–said, "I think he looks angry." And I said, "Well, why do you think he looks angry?" And she said, "Well his arms are crossed and there's red." And then

the Black boy was like, "Well, I don't think he looks mad. He looks confident." And there was like this differing idea of—I feel like for me, the little White girl's response was mirroring what I feel like can happen with White people inferring that a little Black boy is mad, just because of their *being,* or something.

Cleo continued by reading the book, in which the protagonist celebrates himself with pride for qualities including being a "difference maker," a resilient skateboarder who gets back up again after he falls, a "scholar," and many more things. The book closes on an image of the boy with a wide smile on his face and the text "I am worthy to be loved."

Cleo's students engaged with the book with their comments, making connections with the strengths the boy was sharing, saying, "Yeah! I like doing those things too!" But the White girl who had initially offered her criticism of the image on the book's cover reinforced her early assessment, saying,

> "I don't think he's being that nice. I think he's saying that he's better than everybody else. It makes me feel bad." And then the other little White girl in my class raised her hand and chimed in and was like, "Yeah. Makes me feel bad. That's not nice." And then I was just thinking, "Oh my gosh, white supremacy smog emerging!"

Cleo was distressed that the only two White children in her class were responding very differently to the book than the rest of her students, none of whom joined the girls in asserting that the book made them feel bad about themselves. She recalled Beverly Daniels Tatum's metaphor of smog to describe the ways that, as a function of living in a world where racism exists, we all absorb its toxicity unless we are taught to see and resist it.

Cleo concluded their discussion of the read-aloud by reminding the class, "It's actually okay for people to say that they're good at things. It doesn't mean that they think they're better than you." However, she left feeling that she needed to do more to intervene in the girl's critique of the Black boy's joy. She decided that at morning meeting the next day the class would go around and share one thing that they are good at. She reminded the class that if they are proud of themselves for the same reason, they could join with the child who was sharing by using the American Sign Language sign for "me too." Cleo deliberately called on a Black girl to begin the sharing. Her intention with the activity was to communicate, "Let's just practice this. Being happy for people."

It is clear that Cleo has invested in strengthening her capacity to be an anti-racist White educator. While we need to address the disproportionate representation of White teachers in the education workforce, we simultaneously need to invest in supporting White teachers to do this work well. If Cleo had not invested in her teaching in this way, she would not have been able to offer powerful planned curriculum about race and racism, and she certainly would have been unprepared to respond when teachable moments about race arose.

It is important for Cleo, and all of us, to approach this work with humility and a willingness to ask for help when faced with a situation that initially feels difficult and complex. In all aspects of teaching, but especially when there are issues of race and identity involved, teachers can give themselves a chance to return to an incident from the previous day or week to offer a new perspective or to give the children a new set of skills to practice.

Eunji's Six-Year-Old Classroom

> *I don't think there were conversations [in my family] about race in America. I don't think they had that lens as immigrants. And then, moving to the suburbs, I knew I was very much an outlier, but no one provided language for me to express those feelings.*
>
> —Eunji, interview transcript

Eunji is a Korean American first- and second-grade teacher who works at St. Harriet's Private School. As a young child, Eunji lived with her family in a multicultural and multiracial neighborhood in Queens, New York. She described her experience:

> My best friend in first grade was Dominican. I had another friend who was Bangladeshi. And I remember one year I had a

> group of friends who were all from Filipino families. I remember living in an apartment complex where there were a lot of different families.... We were all of varying ages, so I didn't see them at school.... But everyone I knew had a different language that was spoken at home.

Both of Eunji's parents impressed upon her the importance of learning Korean language, culture, and history. As she described it, "They just knew that once I started going to school I was going to lose that language.... Here's information about Korea, the history, the culture, this is what makes you *you*."

Like many immigrant families of the global majority, Eunji's parents strove to be able to move out of the city. In third grade, Eunji's parents moved the family to a wealthy, predominantly White suburb in New Jersey. Eunji described how she immediately felt that she was an "outlier." She recalled that the first time she had a strong awareness of being excluded because of race was in high school when she asked a boy a question and he responded, "I don't talk to people with black hair." Eunji returned home extremely upset and her parents brought their concerns to the school. Though the guidance counselor addressed the incident and the boy apologized, Eunji left the experience with a profound sense that "The overwhelming message was 'you are other.'"

After college, Eunji moved to Korea for a year to immerse herself in the language and spend time with her grandparents. She described it as an important experience, but one that left her once again feeling like "an outsider ... an American." Upon returning to the United States, she began working in education. It was because of working in schools that Eunji felt the strong need to increase her understanding of her own racial identity and her place in the racialized world. She recalled her first teaching position at a Black school in the South Bronx:

> I remember one student saying to me, "You're the first White person I've seen." And me thinking, "Huh. How do I explain to this person that I'm not White?" So I think that it was through their comments where I was like, "Okay. Clearly I need to develop a language for this for myself and then develop a language for them."

At the time of our interview, Eunji had worked at St. Harriet's for over ten years. The school is a predominantly White community, both in the families it serves and in the composition of the teaching staff. During her time at the school, Eunji has sought out multiple spaces to explore race and to deepen her understanding of her own racial identity, including attending the People of Color Conference of the National Association of Independent Schools, the Asian Educators Alliance Conference, and a small book group for Asian American and Pacific Islander educators.

Eunji incorporates learning about race through many aspects of her curriculum. Like many teachers, she selects texts that address issues of identity and offer representation of racially diverse characters into her in class read-alouds. St. Harriet's followed the Teachers College Reading and Writing curriculum, which emphasized the use of diverse books in the curriculum. Eunji was inspired by a presentation she attended at the Asian Educators Alliance Conference by a teacher who shared ways to adapt Teachers College curriculum to amplify opportunities for identity exploration in literacy education. Eunji worked with second-grade students to create identity webs, introducing vocabulary that allowed children to map out intersecting aspects of their identity, including race, gender, class, ability, birth order, and more. Eunji explained that she "started the unit with some sort of web, like 'What do you think about the word *identity?*' and 'What makes you who you are?'" The class would revisit the webs as they engaged in new read-alouds and discussions that added to their understanding of the many components of identity. Finally, students completed self-portraits, including details that illustrated these multiple aspects of their identities.

In teaching about race and racism, Eunji has often designed her own curriculum or adapted curriculum provided by the school to tailor it to what she knows about the children in her class. After a successful year working with identity mapping in second grade, Eunji switched to teaching first grade and found that her students that year were not yet ready for some of the complex concepts that she had covered in second grade. At the same time, as part of a growing commitment to equity and diversity work, St. Harriet's purchased the Pollyanna curriculum, a K-12 racial literacy curriculum, and encouraged teachers to use and adapt it as a resource. Eunji reviewed their curriculum for first grade and noticed that the focus was on "community and noticing difference, and it was about kindness."

After reviewing the Pollyanna materials, Eunji designed a supermarket study. The class visited different supermarkets in the neighborhood, interviewed the people who worked and shopped there, and observed the differences in cost at different types of markets. At each store, Eunji asked the class: "'If we have $5, and we have to buy something that the whole class can share, can we buy something at the supermarket?' Sometimes we couldn't." For Eunji, the supermarket study offered a developmentally appropriate way for her first graders to "meet the people in our community and see how they were different from each other and how the storefronts were different from each other." Eunji felt that her class of first graders was not yet ready for discussion of the more abstract language related to identity markers, so she used the supermarket study as a way to lay the foundation for children to notice and discuss differences that they observe.

In addition to her planned curriculum, Eunji was responsive in designing curriculum that addressed expressions of racial bias that emerged in her classroom. During her first year at St. Harriet's, Eunji was working as an assistant teacher in a classroom with a White lead teacher. A parent in the class Eunji was working in shared with the teaching team that another child had called their child the N-word repeatedly, always when the children were out of earshot of the teachers. Eunji shared that neither the lead teacher nor their administrators seemed to know how to respond. She recalled:

> My head teacher at the time felt very uncomfortable. He just straight up said, "This makes me feel so uncomfortable, I don't know how to do this, I don't know how to talk about this." I felt like Admin had a similar response, like, "These things don't happen. These things shouldn't happen." So it was like, "How are we going to address this?" ... So I pulled out books from the library. I think one was written by Julius Lester, *Let's Talk About Race*. And I also shared that experience of being on the bus [in high school] and conversations around that. But it wasn't like a unit.... But that was the first time where I had to think about the fact that, "Oh, no. We need to really talk about this and name this." But it was because something had already happened. And that was a big learning thing for me. We can't just wait for something to happen. We need to talk about it before.

Though Eunji was new to the school and also the person with the least amount of authority in the classroom, the task of developing curriculum that responded to a racist incident fell to her, one of the only teachers at the school who was a person of the global majority. She acknowledged that she felt uncertain about the role she should play in addressing the situation, explaining, "I didn't want to overstep boundaries or whatnot. I didn't know what sort of community I was in." Nonetheless, Eunji felt that the situation could not go unaddressed. She found children's literature that would open up a talk about race and drew on her own experiences with racial bias as part of the curriculum. This experience strengthened Eunji's resolve to continue to develop her capacity to teach about race and racism proactively, rather than reactively.

More recently, Eunji designed a unit on stereotypes in response to an incident in her classroom in the spring of 2021, during a time when the COVID-19 pandemic made anti-Asian hate especially visible. St. Harriet's provides lunch for the students, and on Wednesdays the students get dessert. The meal one Wednesday was Chinese-inspired food, and the students were given fortune cookies for dessert. Eunji recalled, "I overheard one of my students say, 'Don't eat those. You don't want to get the virus.' Like, 'Stay away from them.' And so I was like, 'Okay. Now I've got to do something.'" In response, Eunji designed a lesson that helped the students define what a stereotype is, to identify examples of stereotypes, and to practice, "Is there a way that you can change that stereotype to become a comment that's not a stereotype?" Eunji also introduced the concept of *equity* to her students and defined it in terms that a first grader could grasp, explaining, "It's when everyone feels like they belong or they feel safe." Eunji found an activity online for older children and adapted it to give her students an experience of collectively making sure that everyone in the community felt included and safe. She distributed stickers of different colors and different sizes to every child in the class and then instructed them that without speaking they needed to sort themselves into groups related to the sticker each child had. Eunji recalled that, after the first round of sorting,

> The one student with the one green sticker couldn't find a group. We shared out and they said, "I feel lonely right now because everyone else has a group." And then the students

were like, "I guess she never said that we have to use the colors." So they got to group themselves again, where everyone could have a group. And I remember after doing this activity for multiple days, one of my students was like, "When are we going to do that again? I really liked the sticker stuff." And I feel like I don't have a lot of kids saying that about reading instruction, per se.

Eunji reflected on the impact this work has on her as an educator of color working in a space where both her colleagues and the families she works with are mostly White people. Over the ten years that Eunji has worked at St. Harriet's, she has seen an increase in the school's commitment to diversity in admissions and in providing administrative support for equity work. Through it all she has been fueled by the self-growth that she experiences through engaging in this work. She reflected:

> I definitely get a sense of purpose out of it. I think there are a lot of days where I think . . . maybe I should do something else that's easier. But I really enjoy this stuff. I enjoy these conversations and I kind of feel like, well, we need to get more educators to be willing to do this. To be willing to do this self-work, and to be willing to have these hard and vulnerable conversations with students. If I were to do something else, aside from teaching, would I actually be able to do this day to day? I don't think I would.

Samantha's Seven- to Eight-Year-Old Classroom

Sometimes I say Afro Latina, sometimes I say Latina, depending on how I feel. But when I do check off race, I check off Black. Anything that asks me, I check off Black. I am a mom to three boys. And I always say I am a mom to three boys of color.

—Samantha, interview transcript

Samantha is a second- and third-grade teacher at La Casa Public School. Though she was born in New Jersey, Samantha grew up with her mother and siblings in Samantha's grandmother's apartment, located near the school building where La Casa is housed today in New York City. Growing up, Samantha was aware that her single mother did not have a lot of money, but their large apartment was filled with multigenerational extended family, joy, and a lot of unstructured play, presided over by Samantha's grandmother, who cared for Samantha and her cousins. In the 1980s, when Samantha came of age, her predominantly Black and Latine community was ravaged by drug addiction as well as the violence that accompanies the illegal drug trade. Samantha recalled that news would travel fast when the "block was hot," and she, her cousins, and their friends were rarely permitted to play outside.

While Samantha was always aware of living in a racially segregated world, the stress of racism has taken a greater toll as she has worked to raise her sons and to keep them emotionally and physically safe and healthy in a world where violence is regularly inflicted on boys and men who are people of the global majority. When discussing her unwavering dedication to being an anti-racist educator, Samantha's voice catches with emotion as she explains that the work is grounded in her experience as a mother. Samantha's continual work to develop anti-racist curriculum is grounded on what she knows about the children and adults she teaches and learns alongside.

Samantha teaches in a combined second- and third-grade classroom at La Casa Public School in Manhattan. Located in a neighborhood with a substantial Latine population, La Casa uses a dual-language model, alternately providing instruction in Spanish and English for half of each day. Additionally, every classroom follows an Integrated Co-Teaching model and includes a percentage of children who receive special education services. Each class has two teachers, one with a general education background and one with special education training. School staff describe the school's philosophy as having four pillars: progressive, dual-language, inclusive, and anti-racist. When the school was founded, the focus was on the first three pillars, but recently school staff have committed to the fourth pillar of anti-racism, in response to circumstances both inside and outside of the school community.

Samantha was one of the first teachers interviewed for this study, and I piloted my questions with her nearly two years before I interviewed most of the rest of the teachers. Two years later, I interviewed Javier and

Matthew, two other educators working at La Casa. Having these snapshots of the school's work over time, I was able to see how their commitment to anti-racist teaching was strengthened over the course of those two years. When I first interviewed Samantha in 2019, she shared with me an issue that she had recently brought to her principal. While Samantha felt strongly that the school served many families well, she was deeply concerned that a number of Black and Afro-Latine families had left the school. By the time I interviewed Javier and Matthew in 2021, Matthew had been recently hired to focus on strengthening the school's capacity to do anti-racist work. Additionally, a new assistant principal with a strong background in anti-racist education had been hired, and the school was working directly to address the concerns that Samantha and others had raised about the experiences of Black and Afro-Latine families at the school.

Many progressive schools like La Casa recognize the benefits of having students work with a teacher for more than one year and in a multi-age setting. This strategy especially supports the Integrated Co-Teaching model that the school uses, in which every classroom includes a percentage of students who receive special education support services. Every year Samantha and her co-teacher design curriculum that allows their students to explore race and other aspects of identity and to envision themselves as agents of change in making the world a more just and equitable place.

Like many of the teachers I interviewed, Samantha uses children's literature to highlight the accomplishments of figures from the past and the present who have contributed to culture and history. Beyond the few that are most often cited, such as Rosa Parks and Martin Luther King Jr., the class studies trailblazers who have worked in a variety of fields, including Angela Davis, Malala Yousafzai, John Lewis, Gwen Ifill, and Roberto Clemente. The students then choose a figure to research and develop a presentation of that person for a "living museum" that families are invited to attend. Because Samantha's classroom is one in which children's multiple modes of expressing knowledge are honored, the children can share what they've learned in a variety of formats. One student Samantha worked with for two years had developmental disabilities that made a written or oral presentation challenging, so she performed a dance to convey what she had learned about Raven Wilkerson, one of the first Black ballerinas to perform in a mainstage ballet company.

In addition to introducing the children to these heroes, Samantha and her co-teachers help the children to understand race and culture by sharing stories of their own life experiences. She recalled the class discussion of a read-aloud from a book about a child in conversation with his grandfather:

> The grandpa was telling the child in the book how they would go down to the river and how they would use the washing board and how they would go to the outhouse in the back and do their business there. And I was like, "Oh I remember at some point when I went to the Dominican Republic as a kid and I had to do this. I never did the washing by the river but I had to go to the outhouse." And then a lot of hands went up. And I was surprised. And they were like, "I did that!" And I said, "Oh, when you went to [the Dominican Republic]?" "Yeah, even in Mexico." ... So we started to talk about it. And I had one child Isaac, he's White, so his hand went up and he said, "I've never had to do any of that!" And I was like, "It's okay. It's okay. We all have different experiences. We all have different things in our life. So it's okay."

Samantha sees the benefit for her students to be part of a multiracial and multicultural community. Education has many purposes and goals. We work hard to help children develop academic skills they can build on as they grow. We can also create opportunities for them to be in relationship with others who have different identities and experiences. Strengthening their capacity for showing up with pride and supporting equity in a diverse community is equally important in preparing children for their futures.

Samantha has witnessed how powerful it is for the children in her class to learn about the fight for racial justice. She recalled a day when the class was reading a book about Martin Luther King Jr.:

> In the reading it said, "Black and White people couldn't sit together, couldn't be in the same school." At that moment when I said that, I had one of my White student girls and one of my Black student girls reach out to each other and hold hands. ... So I stopped and I said, "What led you to do that?"

And they said, "Well, we've been friends a while, and we're best friends." And they really are. And they were like, "I can't picture being in this classroom without her." And, "What happened back then was not fair. And why didn't people do anything about it?" So then we got into the conversation about how it was hard for people to do anything about it.

The painful past and present history of racial violence can be very difficult for children and adults of all ages to process and reckon with. This is why it is important to Samantha that she offer her students the opportunity to envision the role they can play in making the world a more just and loving place. The children write and draw about the ways that they are already leaders in their classroom. These projects are mounted in the entrance to Samantha's classroom and allow the children to publicly celebrate themselves by sharing, for example, "I'm a leader because I help my friends."

During the 2020–2021 school year, despite the challenges of teaching during a pandemic including many months of remote school, Samantha expanded on her previous anti-racist work to offer a year-long curriculum on bias and rights for peoples of all kinds of intersecting identities. The students learned the history of various movements for civil rights, both in the United States and beyond, including rights related to race and gender. The class discussed the structures of democracy and what strategies are available to people when they want to advocate for greater fairness. The children drafted letters to people in power demanding a younger age for voting rights and for reunification of immigrant families. As in previous years, they continued to learn about the lives of individuals who have fought for justice and had opportunities to place themselves in that powerful lineage. They drew, painted, and acted out portraits of the people they learned about. Samantha noted that during free time she observed many of the children experimenting with making different versions of Black Lives Matter posters, in both English and Spanish. The children mapped the aspects of their identity using visual webs and completed multiple self-portraits that allowed them to celebrate and affirm their identities. They interviewed their families to learn about the origins of their names and their family histories. When completing KWL charts (which document what we Know, what we Want to know, and what we have Learned) students posed questions like, "Who invented race?" and "Why is race a thing?" These questions provided the framework for Samantha and her co-teachers to develop more curriculum that pursued the students' emerging questions. In a written piece titled, "What I Think About Racism," one of the students concluded, "If you accidentally do or say something racist, notice it and point it out." Through this deep exploration, Samantha's students have gained a level of humility and accountability in addressing the topics of race and racism that few adults have.

Samantha presented her anti-racist curriculum to a group of educators at a summer teaching institute in 2021. She also shared examples of the children's work. One of the things teachers participating in the review commented on repeatedly was how much joy was evident in the way the children engaged with these topics. Additionally, while many adults worry that children, especially White children, might come away from these educational experiences stuck in a feeling of guilt or shame, Samantha's curriculum offered the children the opportunity to feel the power they hold to take action and to bring about a safer and more equitable world for all of us. Samantha's students clearly came away from these studies with a sense of validation. When completing an identity map that offered written prompts for the students to respond to, one of Samantha's students completed the following responses:

PROMPT: How do I look?

RESPONSE: I look just right. I have brown skin and I always wear two puffs.

PROMPT: What do I believe?

RESPONSE: I believe that everyone should be treated equally.

Samantha also came to the summer institute with questions of her own, seeking ideas she could bring back to the classroom in the coming year. One of the big questions she asked the group to respond to was how to address parent concerns about anti-racist curriculum. She reported that most families were enthusiastically on board with her plans, but one family raised objections, first arguing that children would find the topic boring, and then sharing that they felt the children were too young to learn about these issues.

With the support of school administrators, Samantha met with the family to discuss her plans to approach the topics in a culturally sustaining and developmentally appropriate manner. Following a suggestion made by another participant at the summer institute, she also brought samples of work from the previous year to share on curriculum night with families. Looking at the children's work helped reassure parents that the study of these topics neither harmed nor shamed the children, but instead affirmed their identities and validated their power to fight for justice and equality.

In the next chapter, we will explore further strategies teachers have used to talk to parents about curriculum that addresses race and racism.

CHAPTER 5

How We Talk with Families About Race and Racism

Working with parents was maybe the hardest thing I had to learn in this job that I never felt prepared for with school.

—Lara, interview transcript

I had a kid in my class one year and her mom was like, "She's really happy that you're her teacher because you look like her." And that was really special. Because I never had a teacher that looked like me, my whole school career. I'd never had a teacher who was the same ethnicity as me, or had the same cultural background as me. And to make that connection with somebody, and to see yourself as a grown-up in this room, is really important to me.

—Jasmine, interview transcript

In previous chapters, we learned how educators skillfully weave opportunities for teaching and learning about race and racism into their work with young children. In this chapter, we will explore the complexity of engaging with families around these topics. Many of the educators I spoke with for this book, along with others I have spoken with in the past, have felt generally unprepared for the essential but sometimes challenging work of fostering mutual and respectful relationships with students' families. When I was a new teacher myself, this dynamic caused me the most sleepless nights. Many teachers enter the profession because we love working with children. We quickly come to realize that to be successful in our work with children, we must also build meaningful relationships with their families.

Building connections with families is part of the necessary, joyful, but sometimes challenging work of teaching young children. Bringing discussion of race and racism into the mix of those relationships can increase the potential for both connection and conflict. Tension can arise, especially when these relationships are being built across the spaces of difference that can exist when families and educators do not share a common racial and cultural identity. The stories in this chapter capture some of those moments of connection and some of those moments of conflict.

Trust is the foundation of mutual and respectful relationships between families and teachers. Building trust is essential, especially when preparing to talk about topics that elicit strong feelings, like race and racism. However, power dynamics between families and educators can disrupt this sense of mutual respect. Some families view educators as the experts, and tend to cede power to the teacher in making decisions related to their child's education (Valdés 1996). This is a generous stance, but it can result in educators missing opportunities to learn from families, especially from the cultural funds of knowledge that all families hold (Moll et al. 1992). Families know their children better than anyone, and educators should invite an exchange of their valuable knowledge as it will provide them with information necessary to work well with the children.

Other families, particularly those with racial and economic privilege, tend to assert their power, displaying an air of entitlement and superiority when interacting with teachers. I have witnessed families with little to no training in education persist in instructing teachers about how they should be teaching. These families typically advocate for changes they feel will benefit their child, with little consideration of the impact on the class as a whole. Conversely, educators need to consider how every choice they make affects the growth and learning of *all* of the children in their care.

Even as these challenging dynamics come into play, educators need to invest in finding ways to develop relationships with families, relationships that honor and respect the knowledge and care that all families bring. The following stories provide examples of how to invite families into this vital partnership.

Building Trusting, Mutual Relationships with Families

Several educators I spoke with shared how they drew on their own background to build trust with families. Lara, a White prekindergarten teacher, found it helpful to let families know about her own family history. Lara and her siblings were raised by a single mother, and her half-sister's father is Puerto Rican. As a child, Lara grew up in a multiracial community. She explained that she feels that sharing her own personal history helps families to see her as a whole, complex human being and that this contributes to building relationships. Lara reflected,

> Whenever I have been able to bare myself to families, then they're like, "Okay I get it. I trust her. I love her...." It's the only way I've ever built trust with families is to be like, "This is me and this is my family." And then it just changes the whole dynamic.

Lara felt that sharing something of her own personal identity and history helped her strengthen connections with families, even when they did not share the same history or racial identity.

Jasmine, a West Indian prekindergarten teacher who teaches at the Green Public School with Lara, reflected on the ways that her own history and her family's relationship to her early schooling experiences has a tremendous impact on how she works to build relationships with families. The Green School invites families into the classroom to attend family breakfasts with the class several times a year. Jasmine is attuned to the fact that not all families may feel welcomed into the school or classroom. She recalled that when she was a child, her family did not feel a strong connection with school, in part because of differences in race and culture between her family and the school staff. This leads her to think deeply about what she can do to make all families feel welcome in her classroom. Jasmine mused,

> I think about the families that don't show up. Not because they don't want to, but because they feel like it's not a space for them. And they feel like, "This isn't my first language, so

I can't really talk." Or . . . "I don't want to mingle with other families." Because we usually have family breakfasts a couple of times a year. And those families show up at the end, right? Because they don't feel comfortable mingling with other people. They think it's not a space for them. And I think doing this work, a lot of it, has me reflecting on not only how I want to be seen by the children in my room, but how I want to be seen by the families in my room.

Jasmine acknowledged that, as one of the only non-White teachers at her school, she brings a sensitivity to the experiences of families who are people of the global majority. In conversations with other teachers, Jasmine provides insight for her White colleagues about the needs and concerns of families. Shortly I will share more about the ways that families seek Jasmine out as a resource in helping to support their children's healthy racial identity development.

Vivian and Zara both teach at a Neighborhood Early Head Start, a program that has historically served primarily children from recently immigrated Chinese families. Enrollment of Chinese families went down during the COVID-19 pandemic. School staff shared that they believed this drop in enrollment happened because families were afraid to bring their children to school, due to the documented increase in attacks and discrimination against Chinese Americans in the city during that time (Gao et al. 2023). As seats were made available in their program, they reported an increase in enrollment of Latine families from the surrounding neighborhoods. Early Head Start programs have always been guided by a family-centered philosophy and are often housed within community-based organizations that provide a variety of services. Vivian reported that their center sends all communication to families in three languages—Chinese, Spanish, and English—and that they have prioritized hiring staff members who speak families' home languages. Supporting a racially and ethnically diverse school community requires acknowledging the linguistic diversity of the families. Vivian also reported that, in the wake of anti-Asian hate crimes, the center that houses their Early Head Start program offered self-defense workshops for families. Additionally, Zara recognized the role that educators play in making sure families feel safe:

> We do a check-in to make sure parents are okay, because they do have to walk to our location. A lot of families live nearby, so they walk, or sometimes they take the bus or subway. So we do a check-in: "How are you?" "Are things okay?" and things like that. And that's kind of like the ground level of where they are. They don't really share more or share less. We leave it up to them to share, really.

Vivian, Zara, and the other educators at Neighborhood Early Head Start pay attention to ensure the families they serve are feeling physically and emotionally safe, especially during a time when racist hate crimes have been increasingly visible. These intentional efforts are all essential in building trusting relationships between families and schools.

Teachers bring their expertise in early childhood education to their classroom practice. However, especially when we work in culturally and linguistically diverse communities, we can position ourselves with curiosity and humility and a desire to learn about the culture and identities of the families in our classrooms. Teachers who invite families to share expertise about their heritage, traditions, and practices create further opportunities for building relationships. Audre is an African American and Native American teacher at Grasshopper Montessori, a predominantly White school. In keeping with the global orientation of the Montessori philosophy, Audre and her colleagues design curriculum that explores cultures from around the world. She recognized that inviting parents to share aspects of their family heritage, whether Italian American, Irish American, Latine, or other, seemed to make them more eager to have their children learn and appreciate the culture of other countries. Audre indicated that incorporating families' cultural knowledge into the curriculum was done intentionally, to reassure parents that "nothing that we did was . . . so different . . . or made them feel threatened in any way." Other teachers invited families to share how they celebrate holidays and other cultural traditions. By positioning themselves as learners, teachers can shift the power dynamics of the teacher-family relationship to support the development of mutual trust and respect.

In addition to inviting families to share their cultural knowledge as part of the curriculum, educators can strengthen relationships with families by being open to feedback about their curriculum. This is tender work, so it is important that educators feel they can maintain some agency and autonomy in their curricular decisions when teaching content that may make some families uncomfortable. For educators, questions always remain about how to respond to parent feedback if a parent objects to anti-racist or anti-bias curriculum that they have planned. Nonetheless, when an educator is able to hear and incorporate families' feedback about curriculum, this exchange can strengthen their relationship with families. Lola shared her experience revising her planned curriculum substantially in response to a parent's concern. The kindergarten team at the Kellman Public School plans an author study each year on the books of Dr. Seuss. Despite revelations that some of Dr. Seuss's earlier work included racist content, the team decided that some books addressing topics related to equity were important to explore, so they designed a weeklong series of activities that would be common across all of the kindergarten classrooms. Upon hearing about the upcoming author study, an Asian American mother in Lola's class reached out to express her strong concerns about Lola's curriculum related to Dr. Seuss's books. Lola acknowledged the parent's concern and responded that she believed Seuss had grown in his later work. She reassured the parent that the kindergarten team had chosen specific titles thoughtfully and would be avoiding Seuss's problematic work. Nonetheless, the parent objected to any use of Dr. Seuss in the class. Lola was torn, because she and her colleagues had put a lot of thought and energy into designing the author study and she wanted her class to be able to participate in activities alongside the other classes. She recalled that her communication with the parent "felt a little tense and I was like, 'Oh boy,' and I didn't want it to go there. That's when I went to [the principal] and I said, 'Okay. This is what's going on, and this is what I'm saying. Am I handling this right?'" In the end, Lola opted to rewrite the curriculum for the week, and incorporated some alternative books, including *Sulwe* and *Perfectly Designed*, both of which celebrate and affirm race and other aspects of identity that connected to the theme she had planned for the Dr. Seuss study. Reflecting on how the revised curriculum worked with her class, Lola shared:

> We had incredibly rich conversations. . . . At first I was like, "We had this plan, and I don't want to take it away from my kids, and I don't want to change it. . . ." And it was extra

work for me to go and research and find books that I thought would be connected to what we were reading so we could still connect to the activities [that the other classes were doing], but that would be diverse books. So I found those books. And I had such enriching conversations with my kids. It ended up being such an amazing experience.

While some teachers might feel threatened or frustrated when parents raise objections to their planned curriculum, Lola was willing to be open to the concerns and to put the work into adjusting her teaching. When she and the parent debriefed afterward, the parent expressed gratitude that Lola had been open to her feedback and disclosed that it felt especially challenging for her, as a person of color, to bring these concerns forward. Lola identifies proudly as half Mexican and half Jamaican, but because she has light skin, people sometimes read her racial identity as White. Thus, she herself has had to navigate the complexities of how her racial and ethnic identities are perceived. Realizing that the parent might not feel understood, she shared:

> "I understand. I understand. I completely get it. And I think that as a minority, as a parent, as a person, sometimes it's hard to do that, right?" So I think it was good that we were able to talk about it, that we had the gates open for communication. And it ended up going really well.

Both Lola and the parent seemed happy with the outcome of this exchange, most importantly because it yielded a valuable opportunity for the children in Lola's class. Lola's openness to the parent's feedback developed trust in that relationship.

Lara shared a story of how her perspective on her curriculum was expanded through receiving feedback from a parent. Lara is a White prekindergarten teacher at the Green Public School. She described her conversations with a family in her class who had migrated to the United States from Burundi and Rwanda. The father shared with Lara his critique of how African American history is taught in the United States and how his children experienced this curriculum. Lara shared:

> He was really shocked by how schools talk about race and racism. A thing that I remember him saying that has really stuck with me was that we teach history because we're supposed to, but the history that we teach about racism is really dark and sad. And that that means that kids are learning that all of their Black icons and Black heroes that did things in the civil rights movement all had to die for their beliefs. And if that's the only history that you're learning about Black people that are famous and Black people that were part of movements for any kind of social justice was that they had to die for what they believed in, and for believing in equality or for believing in the movement of Black people, then what does that make Black kids feel like? And he was like, "We are not African American people." They came to America. They have a very different perspective on race and this is what they're learning about race here and about how we teach it.

Hearing this perspective was transformative for Lara and led her to recommit to ensuring that when she teaches about history and the contributions of people of the global majority in the United States she offers children examples of people who have thrived. She reflected that in receiving this feedback,

> It only reaffirms some of the stuff that I was doing, but made me need to do more. Like have a lot of really important Black figures in art and in history present in the classroom. People that are alive that are obviously doing something radical because of who they are, but who are people that are alive that we can still celebrate. And it doesn't have to be a sad end of the story for them.

Lara's experience with this family reminds us that, as teachers, we can always gain insight from being attentive to families' perspectives. While educators bring our strong knowledge of children and curriculum to our work, when we cultivate mutual respect and open lines of communication with families, we can gain valuable insights into how our teaching is experienced by children and families. This is especially important for those of us who are White teachers, whose privilege and life experiences often leave us with a limited view of issues of race and racism. Additionally, being receptive to families' perspectives supports the development of strong relationships between teachers and families.

Finally, teachers can build trust with families when we make it clear that we hold high expectations for all children and their growth and learning. Far too often schools have failed to provide a high-quality education for children of color. There is much talk of the so-called achievement gap, and the language used to describe the difference in educational outcomes for children by race, particularly standardized tests, seems to place the focus on deficits in the learners. This framing is problematic and inaccurate, and many have argued that we should understand this to be an issue of an opportunity gap or resource gap. Too many schools and too many teachers hold lower expectations for children of the global majority and children living in poverty. Even when teachers communicate to families that they care for their children, when they simultaneously communicate a lack of belief in the capacity of every child to learn, they are showing families that they are not deserving of the families' trust and respect. Samara, an assistant teacher who identifies as Middle Eastern, recalled witnessing the feedback that an African American teacher received from a child's guardian in a class of all African American students. She recounted,

> The child's guardian said, "I love how you're teaching them. I love how they're learning." Because the teacher was saying, "You have to get your education!" . . . I don't know what brought up the topic, but one of the children's guardians heard it. And she just said, "I love how you're teaching them and how you're putting this inside, planting these seeds inside their heads."

Samara was witnessing the impact of seeing a teacher who models what Lisa Delpit has described as a "warm demander" (2013). Delpit has documented teachers who combine high standards with a loving stance toward all their students who create the conditions for African American children to be successful in school. In addition to producing positive outcomes for learners, a teacher who communicates high expectations for her students demonstrates to families that she can be trusted to teach their children.

Talking with Families About Race

We must do a better job of preparing teachers of all races to teach and learn with children and families about race and racism. But we also need to do a much better job of making sure that the people who are teaching our children reflect the racial diversity of the children and families in our schools. Several teachers interviewed for this book reported hearing from families who were deeply grateful to have their child learn from a teacher who was a person of the global majority.

Alvin was a retired African American teacher who worked for decades teaching two-year-olds in a predominantly White private school. Though he rarely explicitly addressed race in his work with the children, he recognized that his very presence as an African American man in an early childhood classroom offered the children and families a powerful opportunity to grow in their racial identity development. He recalled particularly poignant conversations he had with families. In one case the child had an African American mother and a White father and the child had very light skin. The mother confided in Alvin how painful it was that people routinely assumed that she was the nanny for her own child. It is well documented that weathering racial microaggressions like this takes a toll on the mental and physical health of people of the global majority. Alvin, himself an African American person regularly navigating the challenges of being in a predominantly White school, was in the unique position of being able to validate the pain of these experiences with the mother.

In another instance, Alvin recalled that a family with a White mother and an African American father sought his advice for how to support the healthy racial identity development of their child. As well, the mother sought support from Alvin about how to metabolize the racism that was now made visible to her as a parent. He recalled,

> I remember in the conference the mother was originally from North or South Carolina. And so she would often talk about experiences on the plane or traveling and would comment on the snarls and the looks that she would get when she was carrying her child with her. So she asked me about it in the conference. And I just said basically the only thing I could say to her, which was that "You will have your own experience

with race. And your child will have her own experience with race." I said, "There's no prescribed answer I can give you on that. I mean there's things we experience collectively and then there's things we experience very individually." ... So I said, "Just arm yourself and get ready. Because it's going to be difficult. But you already know that." And she knew that. So I just basically confirmed what she was going through.

In addition to providing this family a supportive and welcoming learning environment for their child, Alvin was able to offer much more. As an African American person who had endured racism both growing up in the Jim Crow South and in contemporary New York City, Alvin was able to make space for the White mother of a biracial child to process the pain and harm that many families of the global majority experience in a racist world. While no one, including Alvin, could offer this family a solution to the problem that plagues us all, he could validate their experiences with a level of authenticity that simply would not be available to a White teacher like myself.

Jasmine, a West Indian prekindergarten teacher at the Green Public School, shared several stories in which her perspective proved to be an invaluable source of comfort and support for the families of the global majority she worked with. Given her own life experiences with race and racism, Jasmine brings a complex, nuanced view of these issues and a deep commitment to supporting young children's healthy racial identity development. She recalled her close work with a child who was half Black and half Puerto Rican, who at a young age had already begun to internalize painful negative messages about race and identity. Jasmine described a series of conversations she had with the child's Puerto Rican mother about her deeply conflicted feelings when the child asked to have her hair straightened. Jasmine worked in partnership with the mother to provide affirming messages about the child's identity both at home and in the classroom. She recalled, "I had a lot of talks with that mom about how we could build her [child's] self-esteem, what kind of positive self-talk we could have with her." Additionally, they worked together to manage the conflicting goals of offering children autonomy over their own bodies, while being concerned that the child's desire to straighten her hair might indicate that she had internalized negative messages about her Black identity. Jasmine and the mother wrestled with this tension together in a series of conversations. Jasmine explained,

> We talk a lot about consent in the classroom. Like, "It's your body, people have to ask consent to touch you or to do things." And I send a weekly email home to families and I keep them up-to-date with the conversations that we're having. So, her mom was like, "It's her body, she's making the choice for it, I don't want to teach her that she wants something to happen but I have control over her body, because I'm the mom so it won't happen." ... And I said, "Yeah, that's really difficult. I also don't have the answer for that, right? Because we are teaching them about consent, but you are her grown-up and she's asking for her hair to be straightened."

In this exchange it is clear that Jasmine brought her nuanced understanding of these issues in partnering with the child's mother. Jasmine's lessons about consent are especially important in a world where women and girls of the global majority are particularly subjected to regular assaults on their bodily autonomy. As a woman of the global majority herself, Jasmine was able to grapple with all the issues contained in this experience for the mother and child. In the end, the mother offered the child the experience of straightening her hair for her birthday. Jasmine described how she responded on that day and going forward,

> [The child] came to school and she was so happy. She was the happiest she had been in weeks. She was wearing this beautiful birthday outfit and her hair had been straightened. And I remember the para and I said, "Oh happy birthday! Your outfit is so beautiful." We were giving her all this praise. And then she was like, "But look at my hair." And I said, "I was just going to get to that, your hair is so long like this. I noticed that you've straightened it." And I said, "Your hair is beautiful. And I can't wait to see it when it's back in its curls, because those are also beautiful." I remember her freezing and saying, "What?" So I said, "I also love your curls. Your curls are also beautiful. Your

hair is beautiful every day. That's why I didn't remember to mention it. Because your hair is beautiful every single day."

Jasmine knew that in addition to affirming the child's identity in the moment, she would need to provide ongoing reinforcement of these messages through the curriculum in partnership with the child's mother. She explained,

> Then it was a lot about finding books that talked about hair and talked about skin color and making sure that we were giving her a lot of positive self-talk. Some of those meetings with her mom were really good. She said, "I can see that the conversations you're having at school are having a positive effect on her, based on what she's coming home and saying." And I gave the mom a list of books that they could check out from the library or that she could buy that we were reading at school so that she could read them at home.

So much is contained in Jasmine's description of her work with this family. First and foremost, this story reaffirms for us all that we must be prepared to address race and racism directly in our work in early childhood, as it is clear that young children internalize negative messages related to their racial identities. If we do not work in our classrooms to counteract those messages and to affirm every child, we are not fulfilling our obligation to support young children's growth and learning. Like Alvin, Jasmine was able to offer something that all families deserve but not all teachers are able to deliver: a deep commitment to supporting children's healthy racial identity development and a wealth of knowledge gained from their lived experiences as people of the global majority.

Talking with Families About Racism

People of all races may experience great discomfort when talking to others about racism, especially when speaking with people with racial identities other than their own. This is especially true for White people (Jackson and Rao 2022; Menakem 2017). As adults who have been socialized in a world where we have not been expected to practice talking about racism, families and teachers may resist talking with each other about these issues. This means that we miss out on valuable opportunities to support each other in finding ways to speak about racism with the children in our lives. Some of the White teachers I spoke with and White colleagues of the teachers of the global majority I interviewed found the topic of racism so uncomfortable that they avoided it altogether.

Candice is a Black and Native American prekindergarten teacher at the Kellman Public School. She is extremely well versed in child development and careful to present issues in a way that is both age-appropriate and grounded in what she knows about the life experiences and knowledge of the children in her classroom. During the summer of 2020, the uprising in response to the killing of George Floyd, Breonna Taylor, and others was marked by daily protests that passed directly through the neighborhood where the school was located. Candice knew she wanted to support her families in helping their children make sense of the intense experiences we were all witnessing. She offered herself as a resource in guiding parents in how to address these issues at home, saying:

> I had a discussion with . . . parents. I said . . . it's scary for a child to see a big crowd and people yelling and not knowing what's going on. So I asked them to have a discussion that you're comfortable with, with your child about fairness. And I don't think at that age, at four years old, anybody should see any news footage other than maybe the weather.

Candice offered her expertise as an early childhood educator to provide guidance and support to families as they responded to the increased visibility of racist violence. While it may have been easier for her to not bring the topic up, Candice saw having these conversations as a necessary part of her work as a teacher of young children.

In contrast, Amelia, a White kindergarten teacher at the same school, seemed to feel uncomfortable about addressing the same events with the families in her class. When I asked her what role she thinks schools should play in addressing issues of race and racism with children, she offered this as part of her answer:

> Do I want to necessarily talk about current events that are not the best with five-year-olds? No, I don't. Because I don't know what parents want us to say and don't want us to say. And we have to make sure we're not necessarily shying kids away from it. But we don't want to bring up things that are going to either make parents upset or even the kids upset, you know, when you're using terms that shouldn't be used with five-year-olds.

Amelia's discomfort and lack of confidence in her own ability to talk about racism is evident here. Though the children she works with are a year older than the students in Candice's room, Amelia argued that perhaps it is too difficult to find developmentally appropriate language to discuss these issues with young children. Because she does not know how to speak about these issues with children, she is also not able to serve as a resource to families. Amelia had shared that her life history is similar to the majority of White people who have lived most of our lives in segregated White-only communities. When we lack fluency in talking about race and racism, this limits the effectiveness of our work in education. To prepare teachers like Amelia to better address these issues with families, we need to offer opportunities for growth through teacher preparation and ongoing professional development. The necessity of this work will be addressed in the next chapter.

The Complexity of Conversations with Families

Cleo is a White kindergarten/first-grade teacher at the Peabody Public School, which she describes as serving a "majority Black and Latinx" community. Cleo recognized that for most of her childhood and early adulthood she, like many of us who identify as White, did not have a very developed understanding of issues of race and racism. It was not until she began teaching in racially diverse public schools that she realized she needed to invest time and energy in learning more about race so she could be a better teacher for children of all races. Cleo has participated in extensive trainings on the topic of teaching about race and racism with young children, but she still reports feeling uncertain at times when incidents arise. Nonetheless, when she finds herself facing a situation that she does not know how to handle, rather than avoid responding, she seeks guidance on how to address it. Additionally, she continually engages in a process of self-reflection to assess whether she is approaching this work in a way that builds relationships with families across spaces of racial and cultural differences. Cleo recalled how she puzzled through a suggestion offered at one of the trainings she had attended:

> I remember I went to that Center for Racial Justice in Education workshop, and one of their presenters had said that when you have your beginning of the year meetings with your families you could ask them, "How do you identify?" And I remember just feeling like, "Hmm, that's a good idea, but I'm not sure I feel comfortable asking right away for some reason." I think because I'm just getting to know them. But then I question myself and I wonder, am I not comfortable because I don't feel comfortable talking about race and ethnicity? Or am I not comfortable because it feels like a private matter and I've just gotten to meet them? And it's okay to feel like it's not the right time to ask. But I thought to myself, if I were a person of color would I feel like, "Yeah, sure, let's talk about it." I don't know. So it's something I'm still thinking a lot about.

As we hear in Cleo's musing, this type of self-reflection can feel messy and uncertain. It is vulnerable work that allows us to grow as teachers, but it is also difficult work to do on our own. As educators, we must seek resources, mentors, and other supports to assist us in wrestling with these questions, because the process of self-reflection strengthens our capacity to do this work.

For families and teachers who do not share a racial or ethnic identity, talking about race can feel especially challenging. Regardless of whether the topic of race is at the forefront of our interaction, because we bring our racialized identities to the conversation, it is always lingering in the room. What follows are a pair of incidents shared by two teachers, Samantha, who is Afro-Latina, and Lara, who is White. As the teachers shared their recollections of these conversations about children's experiences in school, it was clear that they were very conscious of how their own race and the race of the families influenced their discussion.

Samantha shared a story of her work with the family of Isaac, a White boy in her combined kindergarten/first-grade classroom. La Casa Public School, where Samantha teaches, follows a progressive philosophy with a strong emphasis on play-based learning. The teachers measure children's academic development relative to their own growth, rather than the dictates of an abstract set of standards. Samantha and her colleagues conduct authentic assessments to measure each child's development over time and document their observations of the progress of children's learning. She came to this meeting with Isaac's parents ready to share her concerns that Isaac's literacy skills were not progressing. In Samantha's recollection, Isaac's parents responded by saying, "'We don't care if Isaac's not reading. And we don't care if Isaac's not doing his homework.' It was just like, 'No, no, no. I just want Isaac to play all day. We'll be fine.'" While Samantha understood that the family's main concern was that Isaac enjoy school, she found it challenging to have her concerns about his academic learning recognized. She wondered about their dismissal of her assessment as an educator and mused,

> Yes, it's early childhood. Yes, we want them to have the best social emotionally responsive experience. Yes, we believe in project time. But social emotional practice is also being able to help the kid grow in an academic and cognitive way. Especially if that kid is struggling. And I think that is one of those things that I am really angry at myself for not pushing more for the kids who are struggling.

Samantha's frustration with this interaction was cemented when the family tried to justify to her why another child, a Black boy named Amari, had not been invited to Isaac's birthday party. They explained,

> "Isaac didn't invite Amari to his birthday because Amari's annoying." Mind you, Amari's the Black kid who's in love with Isaac. And I was just sitting here like, "What?!?" But I was just like, "Okay, sure. Okay. Fine." And then afterwards I was just like, "God, why didn't I say something?"

Samantha expressed her frustration that a family who asserted their concern for their child's social and emotional development was also giving their White child permission to exclude a Black child. Yet she was equally frustrated with herself for not pushing back against the family's assertions, which contradicted her knowledge as a teacher. It is not clear whether Isaac's family intended to leverage their racial privilege when dismissing the concerns that Samantha raised, but it is clear that Samantha felt that the family was not hearing her.

Lara, a White teacher who was teaching kindergarten at the time, recognized that her race presented a barrier to her communication with a Black mother when she needed to raise concerns about a child's academic progress. Malik had not attended prekindergarten as many of his classmates had, and Lara had assessed his learning to be behind what he might need to progress successfully in first grade. During the parent-teacher conference she offered Malik's mother the option of having Malik repeat kindergarten. Lara recalled that the conversation immediately felt charged, recounting:

> She was very upset with me. But it seemed like she was afraid to break that racial barrier discussion with me, because I was her son's White teacher and she didn't know how to start it. And I remember my face being hot because I was thinking, "She is so mad." And I didn't realize how I was going to upset her even offering this. Because obviously some people ask for [their children to have the opportunity to repeat kindergarten]. But for her it was offensive.

It seems likely that as they sat down to talk, Malik's mother brought into the room her awareness of the ways Black boys are continually harmed by the system of public education, a system which fails to see their promise and potential (Noguera 2003). It has also been documented that educators disproportionally refer Black and Latine children, especially boys, to the system of special education (Harry and Klingner 2022). As Lara became aware of the intensity and source of the strong reaction, she continued,

> I remember having to breathe, to take a breath. And I said, "I can see why you're getting upset. I know that your perception

of this must be something along the lines of: you're going to have the only Black son getting left back. Although I don't believe repeating a grade means getting left back, you're feeling conscious that that's what it could look like to other people."

By naming the issue clearly and validating a mother's concerns about how her Black boy was being treated in school, Lara and Malik's mother were able to find a way to move forward together in supporting Malik. Lara reflected that as soon as she offered this acknowledgment she could see the mother's tension subside a bit:

> The release that she had in her shoulders. . . . Because clearly we were both sitting there really tightly wound up and dancing around this subject of what she wanted to say and was so angry about but didn't feel like she could say it to me. And then I sort of popped the bubble. . . . And our relationship got a whole lot better after that conversation. But it was really huge, because for her it was like, "Now you finally see me."

Lara's story recalls the work of Sarah Lawrence-Lightfoot's seminal book *The Essential Conversation: What Parents and Teachers Can Learn from Each Other* (2004). Lawrence-Lightfoot reminds us that whenever parents and teachers sit down across from each other, they bring all of their life experiences and identities into the classroom. In Lara's analysis of the situation, it seemed that Malik's mother did not feel safe expressing her frustration to Lara because she was aware of Lara's identity as a White woman in a position of authority over her son's education. All of these realities entered the room and took a seat alongside Lara and Malik's mother as they met. If Lara had not been aware of and able to acknowledge the ways that race was a factor in producing this tension, she might have reacted very differently when she perceived that Malik's mother was becoming upset. When she was able to name the role that race and racism might play in the consideration of Malik's schooling, Lara and Malik's mother could move forward in partnership to address these concerns.

White Parents

No matter the race of all parties involved, the relationship between parents and teachers has the potential to be tender, fraught, and challenging. Teachers of all races might find that White families bring more resistance to addressing issues of race and racism (Cole and Verwayne 2018). Ruth recalled her work with a White mother some years ago who expressed her unhappiness that Ruth was reading books in her first-grade class about Martin Luther King Jr. and Rosa Parks. In response, the parent told Ruth:

> "We don't see color. My daughter never noticed it." And she was very upset that I had talked about race.... That we were talking about segregation and all that stuff.... I guess I was really surprised. And this child had an African American nanny. And I guess they taught her not to notice.

Lara, a White teacher also working at Green Public School, has also faced resistance from White families who question how she addresses the topic of race and policing with her class. She recalled that the family told her they were uncomfortable that she acknowledged, in light of the increased visibility of police violence against unarmed Black people, that some children in the class had said they did not always feel safer when police are present. She described the pushback she received from a White family who told her,

> "We don't want him to question authority and to think that police are bad." So I said, "I understand that, but you should also understand that there are some families that have to have this conversation about questioning authority, because it's not safe for them. So you being able to choose that for your child, choose *not* to have that conversation, is just showing the difference between what another family, a Black family or another family of color, might need to have this conversation with their kids, because they're seeing it and they're hearing about it, and their skin color matches the person who's died."

Lara reminded the family that not all families have the privilege of keeping their children safe from the ugly truth that the system of policing in the United States has produced disproportionate amounts of violence against people of the global majority.

Jasmine also has experienced defensiveness from White families when she has needed to raise issues of race. One year she observed a group of White girls in her class who never played with any of the children of color in the classroom. In addition to observing exclusion during play, one day Jasmine overheard a White child refusing to hold the hand of another child on a walk to the local playground, when the children were encouraged to hold hands with a partner for safety while crossing the street. The child explained this refusal by saying, "I don't want to hold his hand because his skin is dirty." In chapter 4, we discussed how Jasmine addresses incidents like this when they arise in her classroom. Of relevance for this chapter is the resistance Jasmine has faced when she has to speak to White families about these kinds of incidents and issues. She shared:

> What I find difficult is talking to families about it. Like, I'm willing to have the conversation. It's not me finding the will to do it that's difficult. It's that I feel that when I speak to White families about incidents of racism that occur with their children, they're immediately defensive. Because they're like, "Shit, my brown, person-of-color teacher is telling me that my kid is doing this." And then I always get, "But we're not racist. But we're not doing that." And it's like, "I'm not calling you racist. I'm not calling your child racist. I'm saying they have a racial bias. And they're picking it up from somewhere. They're internalizing something, that this person is dirty or I don't want to hold the hand of this person because they're always angry, or they're not listening, or they're misbehaving. And I want to work together to see from both of us how we can, you know, address what's happening, pinpoint where they're internalizing this from, where they're seeing this, so that we can both work together to address it." But I'm very much often met with a brick wall of, you know, "We have friends that are people of color." *(Sighs.)* And I'm like, "That's not the point I'm trying to get at."

It is challenging for a teacher of any race to speak to families of any race when incidents of racial bias arise in the classroom. However, in my experience of working in education for many years, I have found that White families are often resistant to being held accountable when they or their children exhibit racial bias. Jasmine finds this especially challenging as a teacher of the global majority. She shared that she often seeks out advice from her White colleagues about how to speak to White families, because the difficulty White people have in talking about race is so particular to whiteness.

Supporting Families of the Global Majority

In contrast to the resistance some teachers face when speaking with White families, Shu Wen, a Chinese Early Head Start teacher, shared the story of a very productive interaction she had with a Chinese father of a child in her classroom. After hearing a child in her class refer to a classmate's African American father using a Chinese word that could be considered a racial epithet, Shu Wen knew she needed to follow up with the child and his family. She recalled that when she brought it up, "The parents ended up kind of apologizing a little bit. I'm not sure how they ended up at home, but I did not hear that from the child later on. So I hope they fixed it. They tried not to use the phrase anymore." In contrast to the incidents Jasmine recounted, in this instance the parent acknowledged their responsibility for the child's use of racist language and seemed to address it with changes to their behavior. Possibly, the fact that Shu Wen shared the same racial identity may have made the father more receptive to the feedback.

Yet while my anecdotal experience working in education for many years has demonstrated that families of the global majority may exhibit greater resiliency than White families when addressing issues of race and racism, teachers should always bring sensitivity when communicating with families of the global majority, who know that they are raising their children in a world where they will be harmed by racism. Ruth, a White kindergarten teacher at the Green Public School, explained that over the years she had heard from several Black parents that they were "very anxious being at the Green School because this was the first time their kids were not in a Black school." Unfortunately, families raising children of the global majority know that whether they are in public or private schools, whether they are in racially homogenous or racially diverse environments, past and current history has demonstrated that their children will face racism during the course of their education. This may come in the form of interpersonal interactions or through racist systems, structures, and practices. Families of the global majority must be vigilant that their children do not internalize these messages and that they have enough affirming experiences at home and at school that give them strength in the face of the racism that they will encounter in the world. Educators must be cognizant of the very valid concerns that families raising children of the global majority bring into their relationships with their children's schools.

Eunji, a Korean American first-grade teacher at the St. Harriet Independent School, is especially attuned to the needs of the families of the global majority she works with. Eunji brings to this work the perspective she has gained through being in predominantly White environments, both as a teenager attending predominantly White suburban schools and now as a teacher. One event that required her to respond took place during the COVID-19 pandemic. Eunji's class was eating lunch from the school cafeteria, and the menu for the day consisted of Chinese food. For dessert the children were offered fortune cookies, and Eunji reported, "I overheard one of my students say, 'Don't eat those. You don't want to get the virus.'" Eunji knew immediately that she would need to develop curriculum to address this incident with the children, which is described in chapter 4. Additionally, she wanted to communicate with all of her families to let them know what had occurred and to assure them that she was developing a curriculum unit on stereotypes in response. But Eunji also felt that she should first reach out directly to the only Asian American family in her class that year. Before emailing the rest of the class, she called the mother to let her know what had happened and to see if she had any thoughts, questions, or reactions to share. Eunji shared the exchange that followed:

> I called her, just out of curiosity, and I was like, "Hey, I want to let you know about something that happened today. I'm thinking about doing this, but I would love your insight and your two cents." At first she was like, "Whatever you do, I will support." But then as days went by she called me and said, "I'm just letting you know, I think that when you told me that at first I was like, I was so stunned I couldn't react.

> Over the weekend I was raging. I was so upset." And I was like, "I hear you, that's why I called you, I wanted to give you a heads-up that we're going to be talking about this and that this happened in your son's class." And she was like, "This can't be just on you. This has to be something that the school talks about." She has two kids in the school. She said, "I'm hearing more and more that these kinds of comments are being made." So I think that based on our conversation I think she moved more to Admin, like, "What are you going to do schoolwide?"

In reaching out directly to this family, Eunji's first concern was that the family know that she was taking what had occurred seriously and that she was seeking to be responsive to their concerns in addressing the incident. Additionally, she found that in communicating with the family, she was able to build solidarity with them to ensure that the efforts to address these issues would not be limited to her classroom.

Luísa is a White, Brazilian teacher married to an African American man. She works with children ages three to five at Grasshopper Montessori Private School. She recalled an incident during her first year in the classroom when a Black child expressed resistance to sitting down next to a White child at circle time. As Luísa recalled, "He said, 'I don't want to sit down because I don't like the color of her skin.'" Luísa worked with the family of the Black child to make sense of what had occurred. She recalled:

> They were really bothered by it. They didn't know what to do. They were very depressed because they said, "That's not the language we use at home. We never said anything like that, but we do talk a lot about the news at the dinner table." So then I do think the child being the sponge that he is, he just soaked up that information. And in my opinion he felt defensive. And that's how I would put it.

While Luísa felt overwhelmed by needing to address an incident like this in her first year of teaching, she knew she needed to support the family as they processed how their child was responding to the increased visibility of racial violence against Black people in the news. Luísa recalled:

It was at a time that Ferguson was happening. So the news was being broadcast all the time. And I think what happened to that Black child was that he felt threatened, because of the conversations he heard at home. We talked to the parents and in fact they were talking about police brutality and how it was targeted to Black people. And I feel like, with that, he only wanted to protect himself. It definitely came from a real place, because it's one thing that we don't want to see in a pre-K class, but it's good that it happened, because it was a teachable moment.

As teachers, we can serve as a resource to families in helping them understand how racism affects children and what families of children of the global majority can do to protect their children from exposure to information that might provoke anxiety and fear.

Continuing to Grow Alongside Families

As these stories demonstrate, often the greatest challenge teachers face when addressing race and racism comes through their communication with their students' families. This is, perhaps, not surprising. As we have seen in the previous chapters, children often have greater clarity to see and take action against issues of injustice. As they have had fewer years of inculcation into a white supremacist society, they may be able to resist the toxicity of racism with more facility than adults who have been steeped in it for years. When addressing any topic, issues of power and trust always come into play in the dynamics between families and teachers. The strong feelings and lack of practice most adults bring when talking about race contribute further to making this work challenging. In the next chapter, we will explore ways that we can strengthen teachers' capacity to do this work. In the meantime, Javier, a White Latino teacher at La Casa Public School, acknowledged that teachers may need opportunities to support their individual and collective growth in racial awareness before joining with families in these conversations. As a bilingual Spanish/English school, La Casa is on a journey to understand what it means for their predominantly Latine community to become an anti-racist school. Javier noted that this journey has needed to begin with work among the school staff first. He explained,

> We're still finding our way. That conversation that we had amongst the staff, we're trying to see if we can have that with the families in some way. We're trying to frame it so that people don't feel—ay, ay, ay, I don't know, how do I say this? Where people don't feel bad about having these biases, right? Because, in our Latin culture—although it's there, right? Like, "I'm not racist." But then again they say certain things or they have certain feelings. And I'm like, "That is kinda racist." . . . In terms of in the school, we're figuring out how to have those conversations where they feel okay with sharing, where people don't feel like, "Oh, I can't believe you feel like this." Where we're having that same personal discovery. So we're in the middle of that. But we do think that that parent piece is super important. It's super, super important.

In the coming chapters we will discuss the ongoing work we have to do to support teachers in addressing issues of race and racism. As the stories in this chapter illustrate clearly, this work needs to address how teachers of *all* races work with families of *all* races.

CHAPTER 6

How We Prepare Educators to Teach About Race and Racism

I would say that as a college student, I'm still learning about it. I'm still learning as we go.

—Lucely, interview transcript

There are a lot of teachers that are racist, but they don't know they're racist.

—Samara, interview transcript

As a teacher researcher and teacher educator, I strive to view the educators I work with through a strength-based lens, acknowledging that we all bring strengths to our work while recognizing that we all have room to grow. As a teacher and teacher educator, if I limit my view of my students to focus on their deficits, it is harder for me to see the strengths they bring. Nonetheless, it is also important to be honest about the ways that some teachers, often White teachers, do harm to all children when they approach teaching and learning about race and racism. If teachers have not had the opportunity to understand their own racial identity and the effect of racism on our society, they cannot be prepared to support children's healthy racial identity development. All teachers need to understand the ways in which our system of education, because it operates in the context of a white supremacist society, reproduces the oppression of people of the global majority and the privileging of White people. As educators, we can work actively to disrupt this cycle through anti-racist practices. But for teachers to be successful at supporting the healthy racial identity development of all children, we must invest in our own development.

Every one of the teachers I interviewed for this book is on a journey to understand race and racism and to grow in their capacity to support children's understandings of these issues. I am on that journey as well, and so are you. Some of us have worked extremely hard at doing self-reflective work about our own racial identities and also educating ourselves about the systems and structures that influence our work. We do this to become better prepared to approach these topics in our work with young children. Some of us are at a very early stage in our journey of racial awareness. In the book *Woven Together: How Unpacking Your Teacher Identity Creates a Stronger Learning Community,* Courtney E. Rose invites teachers to engage in the kind of growth and self-reflection about our own identities that is necessary to strengthen our capacity to affirm the cultures and identities of the children and the families we work with. In her book, Rose offers a concrete process to support this growth and argues that doing this work serves not only our students but ourselves as educators. Rose writes:

> When we develop a culturally responsive mindset, rooted in student-driven approaches that then manifests into a culturally responsive, student-driven learning environment, we shift the entire culture of the classroom to one that is not only more liberating, more welcoming, more engaging for the students, but it's also more liberating, more engaging and more welcoming for us as the educator because we're shifting from something that is rooted in the singular perspective of one individual, which is me the educator, to one that is more collaborative and communal, which invites all of our voices and all of our experiences into the space. (Rose 2024, 131)

Rose reminds us that engaging in this self-reflective process can support us in feeling more joy and success in our work as educators.

Amelia was one of the teachers I interviewed for this book whose capacity to teach about race and racism was underdeveloped. I will take some time now to look more closely at Amelia's approach to this work not as a way of shaming her, but to make it clear that we must commit to developing the capacity of all teachers to teach about race and racism in ways that nurture and heal rather than do harm. I want to explore Amelia's approach to teaching and learning about race and racism because I know that her approach is more pervasive in the field of early childhood education than the more developed approach used by many of the other educators profiled in the previous chapters.

Before I describe her practices in the classroom, it is helpful to understand the context in which Amelia's racial identity developed. Amelia was raised in a predominantly White community in the suburbs of New York City. She takes great pride in her Irish American identity and shared an awareness of differences in White ethnic groups in the area where she grew up. She described her town being comprised of two distinct ethnically White communities, one predominantly Jewish and one predominantly Catholic, and explained that the two public elementary schools in town were segregated by these two White ethnic groups. Like many White girls who grow up to be White women, Amelia always knew she wanted to be a teacher. When Amelia was a child in school, she saw many models that allowed her to envision herself as belonging in that role. In middle and high school, Amelia began to interact with White children who were Jewish and she reflected that this experience helped her to become more comfortable with difference. She recalled:

> [Middle school was] when I first started going to bat mitzvahs and going to different religious events. But, again, it didn't matter because I liked people for who they were on the inside. It didn't matter what religion they practiced, or where they went to church, or what they did after school, or what they did on the weekend. It didn't matter, because as long as you had something in common with someone you were going to be friends with them, and that was it for me.

While middle school offered Amelia the opportunity to interact with White people from different ethnic and cultural backgrounds, it was not until adulthood that Amelia began to interact with people of different racial identities. Amelia completed her teacher preparation at a state college in upstate New York, and she shared that during her teacher education courses "nothing [about race] was ever brought up in any of my teaching courses." Upon arriving in New York City, Amelia's first position was at a school serving predominantly Asian American students in Queens. Subsequently she was hired at the Kellman Public School in Brooklyn, which she described as very racially diverse, a fact that makes Kellman an exception in the highly segregated system of education in New York City. Amelia expressed her appreciation for the opportunity to work at a school where a multiracial teaching staff works with a multiracial community of families.

Over the course of a one-hour interview, Amelia would often conclude an anecdote by sharing: "Our differences make us unique and our differences make us better. When you're able to see other's differences, that makes you a better person too." Amelia's recitation of this phrase offered an inversion of the claim of color-evasiveness (Jones 2025) that many of us, especially White people, have been socialized to express. While recent developments in racial reckoning have problematized the stance of color-evasiveness, it is still not uncommon to hear a teacher say, "I don't see color. I only see kids." In offering this platitude, a teacher seeks to assert that they have no racial bias and that they treat all children the same way. While all teachers should work to resist what Dr. Beverly Daniel Tatum described as the smog of racism, statements like this are often used to negate the very real and present reality that children's and teachers' race *is* visible. Race is an aspect of our identity, and we all deserve to have our full identities visible and affirmed. Because of racism, race has consequences for how we experience the world. When a teacher states that they do not see color or race, it means that they are claiming not to see themselves or the children they work with fully. It means that they may not be ready to acknowledge the ways that we have all been privileged or marginalized because of our racial identities.

Amelia's repeated assertion that she understands that we are all different and that our differences are a source of strength is a step away from the color-evasive mask that many White teachers claim to wear. Nonetheless, Amelia's awareness may fall short of being able to acknowledge the harm that racism causes. When I asked Amelia to describe how she teaches about race and racism in her classroom, I began to wonder about her understanding of race and how it affects her work. I asked Amelia to describe any curricula or activities that she uses to teach and learn about race in her classroom, and she responded, "Not necessarily about race because the kids are only five—not that I'm trying to shelter them, so to speak, from seeing others' differences, but it really doesn't come up in the curriculum that much." Perhaps if Amelia's teacher education courses had addressed the topic of race, she would have learned that children do begin to notice race and to draw meaning about racial differences well before the age of five (Sturdivant 2023; Winkler 2009). Amelia explained that she and her colleagues work hard to ensure the books in their classroom include characters that represent racially diverse children and families. As she continued speaking about how she addressed race in her teaching, Amelia offered the following example of an exercise she used in her classroom:

> I love the apple experiment. Where you show the kids a bad apple, and you talk about feelings based on the apple, like, "Well this apple is dirty. It's brown. It's ugly. It's this. It's that." And then when you show the kids the other apple, you're like, "Oh that one's pretty and I want to eat it and it's so good and it's going to taste so good." And, really, on the inside it doesn't make a difference. Because those are the differences that you see on the outside. And it's a really great visual activity for the kindergarteners because they can see it.

In describing and implementing this activity, Amelia contradicts her repeated assertion that she sees differences as beautiful. In fact, this activity reinforces racist stereotypes by suggesting that the external characteristics of some apples (and, by extension, some people) are "dirty," "brown," and "ugly" while others are "pretty" and desirable. When Amelia volunteered this as an example of how she teaches about race, she seemed entirely unaware of how deeply problematic the premise of her lesson was.

Amelia's willingness to share and praise this activity with me so freely illustrated her inability to discern that a lesson like this reinforces racism and white supremacy and therefore harms children of all races. It is a clarion call to all of us who work in teacher education and professional development of the urgent need for us to prepare teachers to talk about race and racism with the care and complexity that these topics warrant. Further, we need ways to assess whether teachers have developed the capacity to support children's healthy racial identity development. Amelia's unexamined approach to her own teaching about race and racism may be far more prevalent than the anti-racist pedagogy practiced by many of the educators I interviewed. I offer this story as a reminder that we have to do better to prepare early childhood educators to do this essential work.

We have seen that teachers who make a commitment to supporting young children's healthy racial identity development can create classrooms where rich, complex, and nuanced explorations of race and racism are integrated thoughtfully throughout the curriculum. I recognize that the collection of educators I interviewed may be exceptional in their commitment to this work. Most teachers, even if they are aware of the role they have in supporting young children's healthy racial identity development, may have not yet had the life and professional experiences necessary to address these issues thoughtfully. Because we have been socialized in a world that centers whiteness, it is important that White educators, in particular, invest time and energy in personal self-reflection and education in order to be able to engage in this work thoughtfully with all young children. Yet educators of all races must receive explicit training in teaching and learning about race and racism with young children as part of their teacher preparation and ongoing professional development. In this chapter, I will offer recommendations for how we can invest what is necessary to ensure that every educator has the knowledge and skills they need to be successful in this work.

The majority of the educators I interviewed shared that in their college coursework in teacher education, the topic of teaching about race and racism was rarely addressed. This was particularly true for teachers who attended programs outside of a city, like Amelia, who attended a state college in upstate New York. She recalled, "Nothing was ever brought up in college. Any of my teaching courses. A lot of the methods courses were subject based and not necessarily concept or content based." Clearly, teachers need a foundation for how to teach different skills and content. However, I would argue strongly that teaching how to support emergent literacy, or arts, or early numeracy in the absence of a culturally sustaining approach is incomplete. Additionally, teachers who completed their degrees many years ago indicated there was very little coverage of race and racism in their education coursework. Ruth, who completed her graduate degree in early childhood education at a private college in New York City several decades ago, recalled, "I had no training in graduate school about talking about race." She argued that in addition to providing more curriculum explicitly focused on race in teacher education programs, her experience illustrated the need to provide continual and ongoing professional development on these topics for teachers who completed their studies some years ago.

Teaching About Race and Racism in Teacher Education Programs

Educators who had completed their teacher education degrees more recently reported that the topic of teaching and learning about race was addressed in some of their coursework. They had been taught, for example, that expectations of developmental milestones are often culturally based, and that many child development textbooks are based on White and "Western" expectations for growth and learning. (For examples of how early childhood education curriculum and pedagogy often reflect White cultural standards, I highly recommend Iheoma Iruka, Stephanie Curenton, Tonia Durden, and Kerry-Ann Escayg's 2020 book *Don't Look Away: Embracing Anti-Bias Classrooms*.) Increasingly, early childhood education coursework critiques this limitation and offers a more comprehensive view of culturally based variations in child development. This approach supports educators to view children from a stance that honors and respects each child's cultural and family background. Indeed, several educators interviewed for this book reported that their teacher education coursework emphasized the need for teachers to develop cultural humility and to strengthen their capacity to work with racially diverse families. However, they noted that the issue of fostering connections with families was addressed only in abstract terms, and noted that they would have appreciated the opportunity to practice these skills through role-playing or other active means in their teacher education classes.

The educators reported that throughout their teacher education classes the importance of representation in classroom materials was emphasized. Educators were encouraged to build diverse classroom libraries, to have images of racially diverse people on posters and other classroom materials, to have racially diverse dolls and other manipulatives, and to provide culturally sustaining materials in dramatic play. Several of the educators mentioned that the topic of race came up most often in their language and literacy teaching methods classes, a natural place to emphasize the importance of culturally sustaining practices. However, it is unfortunate that few of the educators recalled this being emphasized in other coursework. There may be missed opportunities to incorporate culturally specific practices in, for example, STEM methods classes, where the Funds of Knowledge (Moll et. al 1992) that families hold could be integrated into the curriculum. Finally, some of the educators shared their concern that when issues of race are addressed, they sometimes lack a nuanced view of race in the United States, leaving teachers who do not identify as Black or White to feel that their experiences are not incorporated into the discussion. Interestingly, two White teachers, Jordana and Ewan, offered the view that their teacher training in the Montessori approach emphasized the valuing of global cultures and was the primary place where race was addressed in their teacher preparation.

When reflecting on experiences in teacher education programs, several teachers offered recommendations for teaching and learning about race and racism with young children. Candice, a prekindergarten teacher and an educator of early childhood teachers, shared how she models culturally sustaining practices in the college classes she teaches. Candice recounted: "Many times when I've asked a student [in a college-level teacher education class], 'Am I saying your name correctly?' So many times they're like, 'You are the first person that ever asked me that in this school.' And I'm thinking that's heartbreaking."

As many early childhood teacher education candidates themselves rarely experienced racial affirmation in their K-12 education, it is important that teacher educators offer them an opportunity to experience what it feels like to have their identities affirmed in an educational setting. While attending to the pronunciation of a student's name may seem like a small gesture, it indicates to the learner that their whole identity is being welcomed and valued in the educational space. Too often educators working in K-12 and higher education fail to make even these small investments in making the students in their classroom feel seen and affirmed. Offering teacher education candidates the opportunity to experience the impact of racial affirmation as a learner may strengthen their commitment to take this care when working with young learners. Beyond learning students' names, there are many opportunities to incorporate students' cultural knowledge and racial identity into our teacher education coursework.

A number of the educators I interviewed recommended that early childhood teacher education classes incorporate an exploration of implicit bias and foster understanding of how racial microaggressions can be present in schools. Samara shared that her literacy methods professor had the students complete some of the assessments available in the Implicit

Association Test (IAT) developed by the Implicit Project at Harvard University. Samara reflected:

> I was so shocked because when I got my results. I thought, "I'm not racist." But it was so enlightening to me, taking that survey and finding out there is racism in everyone. And I told the professor, "This is so shocking to me. I didn't know. I thought I was a fair person." But no.

Instruments like the IAT can be very helpful in demonstrating to prospective teachers that, as a function of living in a racist society, we all hold racial biases. Once shown evidence of our implicit bias, we can begin to be accountable in resisting these biases where they manifest in our lives and work. For example, when teachers identify racial bias in themselves, they can have a constructive conversation about how bias may influence how they see the behavior of children of different races and how they approach discipline in their classrooms.

Matthew is not a classroom teacher, but he was hired at La Casa Public School in an administrative role to support both school staff and families in the school's anti-racist mission. He encouraged those working in the field of teacher education to offer teacher candidates the opportunity to reflect on their biases and their motivations for becoming educators. He noted that in movies and television shows, successful teachers working with children of the global majority are often depicted as White saviors who view families through a deficit lens. He acknowledged that it is not just White teachers who fall prey to this savior narrative and asked all prospective teachers to reflect critically on how they envision their role in education and the relationships they will develop with children and families. Reflecting on the prevalence of the savior narrative, Matthew mused:

> Maybe we want to be there because we think we're going to save somebody and rescue somebody out of a tough situation. We need to ask the question, "Why did you want to go into education? Did you watch *Freedom Riders* the other day and now all of a sudden you want to be that person?" And I don't say that with judgment. I used to watch *Lean on Me* as a kid

and think, "Oh my God, I want to be Joe Clark one day." So if [you] watched *Freedom Riders* and you say you want to be that person, I'm not judging you. But, you gotta get to a point where someone pushes you to critically examine everything that comes with that inspiration, and then what that means for you [to] go into the situation.

By acknowledging the flaws in the popular narrative about teachers who work with the global majority, Matthew pinpoints why it is so important for us all to do the work of self-reflection. In examining our inspirations, we strengthen our capacity to develop respectful, mutual, and authentic relationships with children and families of all races.

Matthew offered additional recommendations that could prompt the kind of self-reflective work that is necessary. In terms of racial and ethnic identity, Matthew identifies as Black and Haitian American. He recalled an experience he had while attending college in upstate New York where he met another student, a White woman, who was so unfamiliar with his identity that she repeatedly mispronounced the word Haitian when speaking with him. He emphasized that many of us will benefit from learning to be accountable for our biases and lack of knowledge and reflecting on the impact of these biases on our life and work. He asked that all teacher education programs offer prospective teachers the space to wrestle with these questions, because:

The girl who called me "Hat-ee-ian," somebody like her might be in the teaching program where she's going to go teach a bunch of Haitian kids. So I think there's needs to be—for all of us regardless of where we are—a moment of reality check. I think a big part is asking us to name and unpack our biases and assumptions straight up. If I'm sending you to work in the hood and you've never even been in the hood, what did you grow up thinking about people who were from the hood? Do you feel safe walking through the neighborhood of your school? Why, or why not? What do you believe about people who are on food stamps? What do you believe about government assistance in general, politically? What is your thinking on that? You've never seen Black people. What is your idea about Black people? What is your idea about a Mexican immigrant who doesn't speak any English? When you hear the term *undocumented immigrant* or immigrant with no papers, what does that trigger in you as a person? I think these are the kind of hard questions we all need to go through and process.

In addition to this self-reflective work, pre-service early childhood educators can be supported in their development through concrete experiences both in their teacher education classes and in related practicum experiences. Gabriel, who identifies as Hispanic, credited the internship placements he experienced in racially diverse schools as critical in supporting his capacity to work with children and families of all races. When I asked Gabriel to recall experiences he had in teacher education that were most effective in supporting him to work with children of different races, he explained, "Depending on where you're from, if you've never taught in that neighborhood, or if you didn't grow up in that neighborhood, it's different. It takes time to understand the children. But you learn after a while. You adjust to it." Amelia, a White kindergarten teacher, also offered the suggestion that it would be important for pre-service educators to visit classrooms with students who are racially different from them. She coined the phrase "shelter shocked" to describe how she felt as a novice White educator teaching in racially diverse schools when she had only ever been in predominantly White spaces. When asked what recommendations she had for the field of teacher education, she offered,

> I just think that it's important that future teachers see that kids are different. . . . I wish there could be more like a fishbowl kind of thing, so that even young teachers that are learning to be teachers could see what the classroom looks like before going into it, so that they're not so "shelter shocked" by what they might see.

In sharing this recommendation, I want to make clear that I am not suggesting racially diverse classrooms should be offered up as a laboratory to expand White teachers' awareness. It is critically important that teacher education programs provide pre-service teachers an opportunity to grow in their own racial identity development *before* visiting classrooms. However,

Amelia's point is well taken that educators' first experience in classrooms with children of different races than themselves should happen before they are hired for their first teaching position. Thoughtfully supervised practicum experiences included as part of teacher education programs can let prospective teachers witness experienced teachers offering culturally sustaining curriculum and pedagogy prior to being responsible for their own classrooms. Additionally, many teacher educators incorporate intentional community walks in the neighborhoods where their students are completing their practicum experiences, allowing the pre-service teachers to learn about the strengths, resources, and challenges that provide the context in which the children live.

Many of the teachers emphasized that the most challenging part of teaching and learning about race and racism with young children was not in their experiences with the children, but in their interactions with families related to these topics. When I was a new teacher, I felt especially underprepared to build relationships with families. I had gone into teaching because of my love of working with children, but I quickly realized that my success in working with children was contingent on my capacity to foster relationships with families. Lara articulated what many of the other teachers shared in identifying this as a gap in her otherwise very thorough teacher preparation program. She reflected:

> I feel like I went through my teacher education program and I felt really ready in terms of how I want to teach and how I think kids should learn. . . . The thing that hit me like bricks when I got to actually teaching was working with parents. I felt like that part was always really missing from my education and that [what] I was wildly unprepared for was how to talk to parents and support parents and understand their perspective as a person who is vulnerable leaving their baby with you and trusting you that you're going to be doing whatever important work that you're doing to be raising them.

The challenge of building relationships with families may be compounded when addressing the topics of race and racism, which many adults feel uncomfortable discussing, especially across spaces of racial difference. In the previous chapters I shared some examples of ways that teachers were able to successfully respond to families' concerns about curriculum that addresses race and racism. It is especially crucial that teacher education programs prepare educators for these encounters. In order to provide a foundation for these more challenging conversations, all teacher education programs must strengthen educators' capacity to take a stance of cultural humility toward learning about the cultures and racial identities of families in their classrooms. Especially in early childhood, families should feel welcomed into the classroom and there should be opportunities for them to share their cultural knowledge with the community. By inviting families in as experts, teachers can cede some of their power and authority over the classroom, enabling genuine, mutually respectful relationships between teachers and families.

Vivian recalled that videos were particularly instructive for her during her teacher education coursework in developing her knowledge of different modes of communication and cultural expectations. She recalled a particularly memorable component from one of her teacher education classes:

> They showed a video of different schools in different countries and how you respect the culture. Like in Japan or Asia, you have to take off your shoes to go into a school. That's a sign of respect of the teacher and the school. That this is your home.... Videos from home visits can show there's a lot of nonverbal cues that I think the textbook doesn't do much [to teach about].

Additionally, teacher preparation programs should offer future educators the opportunity to role-play scenarios in which they communicate with families about a variety of topics. One of the strongest and more recurring recommendations that came out of my interviews with teachers was to give pre-service teachers the opportunity for hands-on practice in engaging in these discussions. They explained that often in their teacher education coursework, issues were discussed in abstract terms, leaving them unprepared to respond concretely when those issues arose. The educators suggested that teacher education programs should encourage pre-service teachers to brainstorm about how they would engage with families over various topics, working with scenarios in the low-stakes setting of the college classroom.

As an extension of exploring educators' unconscious bias, it is critically important that teacher education programs provide future educators a space to consider and be accountable for how their biases influence their approach to discipline in the classroom. Teacher education programs should discuss the findings of research (Morris 2018; Noguera 2003) that documents the ways that harsher discipline approaches disproportionately target children of the global majority, even in early childhood classrooms. When I teach a social foundations class, my students and I listen to a segment from the *This American Life* podcast episode titled "Is This Working?" The first segment of the episode documents the experiences of a Black mother in Oklahoma named Tunette Powell, who recounted how her preschool-aged son was repeatedly suspended for engaging in behavior less harmful than that of White classmates who did not receive comparable punishment. The episode expands on this case study by offering national data on disproportionality in school discipline by race. (While Powell was less familiar with the research documenting this issue at the time of these incidents, she has subsequently become a scholar and activist who focuses on these concerns.) Discussing this episode in our teacher education college classroom always results in an engaged active dialogue. It is critically important for future educators to reckon with the impact that our own unconscious bias can have on the children in our care.

Intentional practicum placements are an important component of teacher preparation, with cooperating teachers who model promising practices and mentor pre-service teachers. Jasmine, a prekindergarten teacher who hosts early childhood teacher education students in her classroom, emphasized that she feels a responsibility for addressing these issues with her student teachers. She recounted:

> Something that I talk a lot about to my student observers that come work in my classroom is who's getting in trouble in the classroom. There was an instance of a student observer—it was a down time, we were doing puzzles and reading books and all the kids were engaged in their own thing—and two girls were doing ballerina moves and two boys were flossing.

> It was two different things. And she said, "Oh, aren't you going to tell them to stop?" And she was talking about the two boys. And I was like, "Why?" And she was like, "Oh, well, they're dancing." And I said, "It's really interesting that you think I should tell the two boys who are flossing to stop, but the two girls who are doing ballerina moves don't need to stop."

In this example, there is clearly a gender bias at play as well. We often perceive girls' behavior as being more acceptable than the behavior of boys (Noguera 2012). Additionally, scholars including Monique Morris (2018) have observed that Black girls' behavior is more harshly targeted for punishment than that of girls of other races. As part of the work of preparing educators, we must make them aware of how unconscious biases cloud the lens through which we view children's behavior.

Candice, a longtime prekindergarten teacher and teacher educator, reflected on witnessing current and future educators struggle to understand how their own biases are linked to systemic racism.

> New teachers—or really old teachers who have been there way too long—we see how they are struggling to not feel guilty about racism. But sometimes the feelings that you have of guilt can make you feel helpless, or hopeless, or detached. So I think we need to be able to pull them in, make them understand that, it's not you personally that did this, but we have to realize that you're part of that history that we need to change. And because you're part of that history, sometimes you have a more powerful role, a more powerful capability to change what's going on, you know? So [there's a] question that I had. How can we help teachers not be racist? How can we help teachers teach their children to be anti-racist? To recognize when "Oh, that's something that I was about to say" or "That's something that I was about to think, and that's not right."

While it is essential that all teachers do the individual work necessary to be accountable for and to resist our own biases, we must also understand how systemic racism shapes our lives and our institutions, including schools. If we do not grapple with these realities, we may not be able to grow in ways that are necessary to strengthen our teaching.

At the time of our interview, Luísa had completed four years of an undergraduate degree in early childhood and was one year into her master's degree. She shared:

> To be honest, in my classes we only talk about diversity; we never really talk about, "Oh, and if this happens...." Like, when it happened in my classroom that my Black child didn't want to sit next to the White child, we never talked about the situation in any of my classes. I've been in school for five years now, and we talk about diversity and how we should advocate for a more racial conscious classroom, but I think it's just talking.

Luísa recalled how unprepared she felt when a child in her class said that they did not want to sit next to another child because they were a different race. Responding to these kinds of moments, which arise in many early childhood classrooms, is challenging, and they must be handled with great care and intention. We need to give future educators the chance to practice unpacking what is happening in the moment and then develop strategies for how to respond in a way that is healing rather than harmful.

Additionally, the educators I interviewed strongly recommended that teacher education programs offer future educators the opportunity to practice how to communicate with families about issues related to race and racism. Educators need to practice responding to families' concerns about curriculum that addresses race and racism, and they especially need to be able to practice the process of talking to families when incidents related to race and racism occur in the classroom. Eunji shared several incidents that had taken place in her career when she needed to speak to families when children in her classroom said racist things. Eunji was otherwise very satisfied with how her teacher preparation program prepared her to plan and implement multicultural curriculum, but she recalled that it had not prepared her for how to respond to unplanned interactions.

> There wasn't actually ever a class on "This is how we talk about race." Or even, what do you do when a student makes a comment? When a student is supposedly saying the N-word,

and they know to say it when adults aren't there? Or, what do you do when a student says that a fortune cookie will give you COVID? There wasn't that kind of training. And not to say that there needs to be a syllabus for that, but I think making more space for emerging educators to share, "I experienced this at work today." And having this group to think through and process what that feels like, how to navigate certain hierarchies. What is developmentally appropriate? Any sort of troubleshooting, I think would be so helpful.

Finally, three other recommendations arose during my conversations with the educators I interviewed. These recommendations are not specific to the curriculum and pedagogy in early childhood teacher education coursework, but they are no less relevant to the development of educators. Several of the educators shared that their capacity to address issues of race and racism in their work was supported by coursework that they completed outside of their teacher education credits. They cited courses they had completed in sociology, linguistics, gender studies, history, race and ethnic studies, arts, and literature as being instrumental in raising their awareness about race and culture and the systems that produce injustice. I want to elevate this recommendation in light of the fact that many districts across the country are developing programs that offer a fast track to the classroom to address teacher shortages. These alternative certification programs often rely on having prospective educators complete credits that are limited specifically to education classes. When prospective educators no longer have to complete coursework in other disciplines, they may miss out on gaining the critical knowledge of the world, growth, and self-reflection that these courses offer.

For example, Matthew emphasized that learning historical truths provides an essential foundation for being a good educator. He encourages educators to consider what histories they are learning and whose stories are left untold or incomplete. Reflecting on his own education, Matthew mused:

> When you're giving people texts of knowledge about people who look like them, where does that story begin? And then how does that story continue to evolve from there? I'm never going to say we should not teach slavery and not teach

about the civil rights movement because that would be nonsensical.... But I didn't learn anything about Indigenous people until Christopher Columbus or any of the settlers came over.... So be intentional about the starting point of teaching people about their history ... and then, how does the story build from there? And is there always a triumphant, empowering lens throughout that is consistent, and not one that is "woe is me" kind of thing?

The next two recommendations for teacher education programs as they prepare early childhood educators to teach and learn about race and racism are focused on who is in the room in teacher education classrooms. A number of the educators I interviewed shared that their experiences in their teacher education programs were directly affected by the racial demographics of that program. Ruth, a White teacher nearing retirement, shared that she experienced one of the most profound moments of learning in her graduate school coursework while in a literacy class. One of her classmates, a Latina woman, spoke movingly about the fact that she had never seen any characters that looked like her or that matched her cultural or linguistic identity in the books she read as a child. Hearing the effect that this had on her classmate had a profound influence on Ruth and solidified her commitment to having a diverse classroom library. Samara, an assistant teacher who identifies as Middle Eastern, gained perspective on how even "positive" racial stereotypes act as a microaggression. She shared, "There was an Asian girl in our math [teaching methods] class, and she was like, 'I hate when they say, "'Oh, you're Asian, you're supposed to know math.'" She said, 'That put a lot of pressure on me. I'm not good at math.'" Samara shared this story as an example of how her thinking had been transformed simply by hearing from the perspective of a classmate with a different racial identity from her own.

Jasmine, a West Indian teacher who grew up in the Bronx, shared that she had thought long and hard about which college to attend to study education. She lived close to a predominantly White, private college with a highly regarded education program. However, she chose instead to enroll in her local public university and felt affirmed in this decision because of the racial demographics of both her classmates and the faculty. She recalled:

> I struggled a lot between going to a [public college] and going to [the private college]. . . . I felt like at [the private college] I would be trying to fit in to that culture. Or I would have to mold myself to fit there. And I felt like [the public college] was a place where I saw people that looked like me and I could relate more to that experience. . . . And I had a wonderful time there. I met wonderful people and had really great professors. I was taught by people from all over. It was a very diverse group of grown-ups working alongside me and teaching me, and that felt good. I didn't feel like I was missing out because I didn't go to a different kind of school.

Similarly, Samantha experienced challenges adjusting to the culture of another private college that she attended for her graduate studies that almost resulted in her dropping out of the program. Though Samantha had completed her associate's and bachelor's degrees at public colleges, she was strongly encouraged to attend the graduate program at a private college where many of her colleagues at La Casa Public School had studied because their programs were closely aligned with the school's progressive philosophy.

> When I got to [the private college] I was there on a scholarship, first of all. And then my first class there were some questions asked, like, 'Who has kids?' And I'm the only one whose hand goes up. 'Who works in a public school?' And I'm the only one whose hand goes up. . . . And I looked around, and I was like, well, no wonder. They're all in their twenties, they're all White. I believe they're all Jewish. And I was like, they are all of who I'm not. I'm not White. I'm not twenty. I'm not Jewish. And I have three kids. Grown kids. And I'm Brown. I'm Latina. I can't relate to anybody here. I just can't. And I didn't make any friends in that class. Because that first day I was just like, "Oh God."

The private college that Samantha attended expresses a deep commitment to issues of social justice and seeks to enroll students from racially diverse backgrounds. Nonetheless, due to the racial wealth gap and other aspects of structural racism, many private colleges have historically served a predominantly White student population. Samantha eventually met one other student of the global majority and was assigned a Latina adviser who convinced her to stay in the program.

There are many implications surrounding the pair of stories that Jasmine and Samantha shared. As we know, 80 percent of teachers in the United States are White, yet research has documented the benefits to students of all races in having educators of color (Cherng and Halpin 2016). From the stories shared above, it is clear that current and future educators benefit from being in racially diverse teacher preparation programs. If we are committed to building a teaching workforce that reflects the racial, linguistic, and cultural diversity of children and families whom schools serve, we must commit to supporting educators of the global majority throughout the process of teacher preparation. This especially means that predominantly White institutions of higher education need to be thoughtful about the practices and policies they put in place that encourage or discourage teacher candidates who are people of the global majority from enrolling and persisting.

Further, we must continue to fight to ensure that colleges that serve students of the global majority have the funding and resources they need. One way that all teacher education programs can support the success of teacher candidates who are people of the global majority is to hire more teacher educators of diverse racial and ethnic identities. Samantha attributed her decision to stay in her graduate program to having a Latina faculty member as her adviser. Several years ago, Samantha began teaching as an adjunct faculty member at the community college she had attended nearly twenty years before. She has received very positive feedback on her teaching from both student evaluations and peer observations. She reflected, "I think I was really successful because the students at [the community college]—they look like me and I look like them. Once I say I'm from [the same community college] they're like, 'Oh! I can be you one day!' I've actually heard that from them before: 'I could be you one day.'"

Professional Development

It is critical that early childhood educators have a foundation for teaching about race and racism before they enter the classroom. Yet our learning as educators should always be ongoing. Individually, we grow as human beings, and collectively, society evolves in new understandings of issues such as race and racism. All of the teachers I spoke with shared reflections on how professional development experiences influenced them as learners and as educators. Ruth, a White teacher nearing retirement, underscored how appreciative she was of opportunities to learn alongside her colleagues throughout the course of her career. She reflected, "In terms of educating educators, it has to be ongoing. Because I just feel that from when I started teaching until now, things are very different, in how people are taught and even the materials available." Ongoing professional development on the topics of race and racism allows for new knowledge, materials, and understanding to be incorporated into educators' existing repertoire. Professional development is necessary to address the fact that, after completing their degrees and licensure requirements, many educators are still unprepared to support young children's healthy racial identity development. This is because many educators have not yet reckoned with the ways that our own racial identity and racism influences us and our teaching. Samara emphasized,

> I think a lot more in terms of professional development would be great. Because there are a lot of teachers that are racist, but they don't know they're racist. I've heard teachers in the school that I work in. They have conversations, and you can tell that's racism. But they don't know they're being racist. These are older women.

The field of education is a microcosm of greater society. Because every child deserves to have their racial identity affirmed and nurtured in school, we should be able to ensure that every educator who enters the field is committed to doing this work well. Until we have eradicated racism and white supremacy, schools will continue to reflect these toxic beliefs and structures. Ongoing professional development can offer the possibility for educators to grow in their capacity to support every child's healthy racial identity development.

Of the educators I spoke with, nearly all had experienced some form of professional development that addressed race. The only educators I spoke with who said they could not recall workshops that were explicitly about race were the teachers in Early Head Start Programs serving children under the age of three. While research (Winkler 2009) documents the ways that children as young as six months old seem to be aware of racial differences, the educators of very young children did not describe developing curriculum that spoke explicitly about race. Despite this, the Early Head Start teachers did report engaging in many conversations about developing trusting and respectful relationships with families, which necessitates being attentive to issues of culture and difference.

The rest of the educators spoke about two types of professional development experiences, those that involved having trainers from outside of their schools and programs versus conversations internal to the organization in which teachers worked collectively to expand their knowledge of the topics. In New York City, educators have benefited from workshops with a variety of organizations that focus specifically on teaching and learning about race and racism, including Human Root, the Center for Racial Justice in Education, New York University's Metro Center's Critically Conscious Educators series, and Undoing Racism. Several of the educators working in public schools in New York City also cited trainings offered by the Department of Education, specifically workshops for prekindergarten educators on working with diverse families as well as a series of workshops on implicit bias that was mandated for all public school educators under the leadership of former Schools Chancellor Richard Carranza. Some of these workshops were opportunities that the educators sought out themselves and some were school based. Eunji's school recently hired a diversity, equity, and inclusion coordinator and has demonstrated an increasing commitment to this work. However, in her first years at the school, Eunji proactively sought out spaces that would help her to grow in this work. These included the People of Color Conference sponsored by the National Association of Independent Schools as well the annual conference of the Asian Educators Alliance. Other teachers attended gatherings at Bank Street College of Education, both the annual Teaching Kindergarten Conference and the annual Symposium on Black Lives Matter in Early Childhood Education. Several of the educators mentioned trainings and conferences that were not exclusively focused on the topic of teaching about race and racism, but which intersected naturally with issues of equity and bias. These included workshops on the uses of restorative practices and restorative justice as well as trainings offered by the Transgender Institute. Additionally a number of the teachers I interviewed were active participants in the Institutes on Descriptive Inquiry (IDI). In the interest of full disclosure, I should share that I serve on the board of IDI, which is how I made connections to these teachers. Our work together has always focused on taking a strength-based stance toward children and families, and we have grappled with the ways that issues of race and racism affect how children and families are cared for in schools.

Working with external trainers can have great benefits, as people from outside of the school can reflect back candidly to the community what they see as the strengths and areas for growth there. When hard truths need to be made visible, it can be emotionally taxing to have that happen within a community whose members need to continue to work together day by day. However, often it can be valuable for a school to work collectively on these issues, tapping the internal knowledge that members of the community bring. There are many benefits to cultivating professional development experiences internally, not the least of which is the cost associated with working with outside organizations. Many schools, especially public schools, lack funds to contract with an outside organization. Additionally, it can be a powerful experience for a community of educators to position themselves as learners, building knowledge and understanding collaboratively. This process can allow a school community to focus their professional development in on-the-ground issues that are particular to their school. For example, Javier shared that La Casa Public School tried working with two different consulting groups before deciding to start its own team from among the school staff who would design professional development opportunities that responded specifically to challenges the school was facing regarding issues of race. He was pleased to have the opportunity to join the Equity Vision Implementation (EVI) committee that was responsive to a concern Samantha and others had raised about Black families leaving the school. As Javier described it, working as an in-house team on professional development offered the opportunity of "being intentional to see what we can come up with." Fortunately La Casa's EVI work was a priority of school leadership and included support from staff like Matthew, who brought his deep knowledge of these issues and his commitment to this work.

As with La Casa's EVI committee, several schools established a dedicated working group devoted to issues of diversity and equity. To ground their work in the needs of the school community, they often began by surveying the wider community to identify issues to address. Audre, who served on the Grasshopper Montessori School's newly formed Diversity Committee, described the need for this work as follows:

> There's a lot of teachers who really don't understand each other and it's been going on for quite some time. So we're going to be doing workshops and we're going to be talking about those things openly with teachers and ask[ing] them for their feedback. And following up on their feedback. Whatever their feedback, we'll find another workshop that's related. . . . And just keep that web going until people feel comfortable with each other.

Audre captured the challenges of doing the complex, essential, and ultimately fruitful work as a multiracial school staff. She recognized that before they can truly begin, they will need to invest the time to learn about each other and the life experiences they each bring to the topic of race and racism.

Lara, Jasmine, and Ruth all work at the Green Public School, which uses processes of descriptive inquiry in helping the school staff to have productive conversations about complicated topics. One of these processes is the sharing of recollections, telling the story of a time in each person's life related to a shared prompt (Himley et al. 2002). The Green School staff regularly share recollections in their staff meetings to explore topics that the school community needs to focus on. This structure allows the staff to learn from one another and to gain a more complex perspective on the issues at hand. It also establishes the level of trust and vulnerability necessary for the teachers to share candidly with one another. Jasmine described ways that the school staff regularly learned from each other through formal and informal reflective conversations about their teaching. While there are many people of the global majority on the school staff, many are assistant teachers, and Jasmine is one of a handful of lead teachers of color. She recognized the ways that her White colleagues relied on her to provide cultural knowledge that was important in working with families of the global majority. She shared:

> We try to make sure that we're being responsible to situations that are coming up in our rooms that maybe we haven't

been faced with before or that we don't have perspective on. I remember one situation was, a little girl in a different class got scratched on her face. And I said, "You have to be very sensitive to that family, because a lot of Black and Brown families are unhappy when their daughters come home with a scratch on their face. That's big thing for a lot of families." And they were like, "What are you talking about? She's a kid. Kids get scratched." So I was like, "I know kids get scratches. You know kids get scratches. But this is a cultural thing. I remember if I ever got a scratch on my face my mother would be furious. And that's because it was a cultural thing." So I think it is helpful that when we're sharing, that we all have the perspective that we can impact one another, so that we're still learning from each other.

Ruth recognized that the internal professional development that the Green School staff engage in with each other was instrumental in her ongoing growth as an educator, particularly as it related to her learning about race. When I asked her what impact teaching about race has on her as a educator, she initially responded by sharing candidly, "It makes me feel stupid. . . . It makes me feel stupid that I'm so unaware." But she acknowledged that it had been tremendously helpful for her to gain wisdom from her colleagues because they were able to share more complex understandings of issues related to race and gender. She acknowledged that she wrestles with her desire to learn from them, while also not wanting to place the burden for her growth on her colleagues who are people of the global majority. She summarized this conflict by acknowledging:

> You know you shouldn't ask your colleagues of color because they're already under enough stress, so I don't want to ask, "Am I being racist?" So I try to leave them alone. But then it's like, how helpful are a lot of other White people telling me how racist you are?

Ruth and other White educators struggle to reckon with the ways that White affinity groups can be used to raise racial consciousness for White people while keeping the burden off their colleagues who are people of the global majority. Cleo recognized that much of the work that she needs to do as a White educator is labor she needs to take on herself. Educators like Cleo and many of the other educators I spoke with invest their own time and energy on strengthening their capacity to teach and learn about race and racism. She described that during the summer of 2020 she was part of a small book group comprised of White educators who read Bettina Love's book *We Want to Do More than Survive: Abolitionist Teaching and the Pursuit of Educational Freedom* together. She explained their rationale for a White affinity book group this way:

> We made a little White affinity group online to read it. Not that I always want to be in a White affinity group, because I don't. But I felt that for that book it might have been good. I feel that sometimes to not have to ask any Black colleagues to have to do emotional labor, to have to explain anything, or hear me ask a really dumb question. . . . And also for White people to help each other do better. And I don't want to ask a Black person to help me do better in terms of talking about race. That's something that I have to work on on my own and with other White people who have to work on that. Not that I don't want to learn from colleagues of color, but I don't want to make them feel like they have to teach me. That's what I'm trying to be aware of. Because we were trying to educate each other and take our responsibility for our own learning, which was the idea behind [the affinity group].

Of the teachers I spoke with, one did express some hesitation about how much schools prioritize investing time and money in teaching about race and racism, primarily because of the narrow way that these topics are addressed in teacher preparation and development. Vivian is a Chinese American teacher who was raised in Vietnam until she migrated to the United States at the age of eleven. She is proud to work in an Early Head Start program that uses a "culturally sensitive, child-centered approach." When I asked her what role schools should play in teaching young children about race and racism she raised a critique of the ways in which we address these topics in teacher training. She offered her feelings upon hearing about the New York City mayor's priorities for school funding.

> [The Mayor] wanted to invest in more culturally responsive curriculum. I'm not too sure I agree with that. When I think about it, when I was in school, I think racism was brought up with me as mostly Black and White. We [Asians] are not part of the conversation. I mean I was living it. But in terms of the school, it was always Black and White. That was the subject in terms of racism. So I mean I was listening to it, but I feel like I know that it's happening too, because I live in a very mixed community. I do feel like left out because I was not included in that topic as an Asian American.

As we continued to talk, it became clear that Vivian recognized the need to address race and racism in schools. However, she raised a valid concern about the ways that race is often discussed that do not allow these topics to be addressed with nuance and complexity. When this happens, efforts to be equitable and inclusive may result in leaving some teachers and students feeling marginalized. Vivian's criticism of how some of these conversations have been framed offers an important caution for how we implement this work going forward.

Finally, we might continue to consider ways to intentionally connect early childhood teacher education preparation programming and the professional development of staff in schools used for practicum experiences. The cost of hiring outside trainers can be prohibitive for schools, but many schools host pre-service teachers for practicum experiences. Cleo recalled that one of the most valuable professional development experiences on teaching about race was a series of workshops led by a local early childhood teacher education faculty, who offered the trainings as part of an exchange for hosting student teachers at the school. Many teacher education faculty are themselves overextended and overworked, but it seems well worth exploring the possibility of developing this kind of exchange. Grant-funded programs have experimented with this kind of reciprocal relationship (Garte and Kronen 2020). This model provides benefits to both the school and the teacher education program. Teacher education faculty are invested in supporting schools that model promising practices for the future educators in their college classes. Because teacher education faculty often have a long-standing relationship with schools, faculty can ground the professional development experiences in their knowledge of the school's culture, strengths, and challenges. Many schools lack funding and the human resources required to develop meaningful professional development experiences through in-house staffing. This model would require an investment, but seems like a worthwhile one to experiment with and expand upon.

> **Frameworks for use in teacher education and professional development**
>
> *Defending the Early Years' Fostering Healthy Identity Development in Young Children*
>
> *Center for Anti-Racist Education's CARE Framework*

CHAPTER 7

How We Change the World

As we have seen from the examples shared by the teachers in the previous chapters, young children absolutely are ready to join with us in learning about race and racism. When the teaching is done well, children are not harmed or shamed or traumatized, but instead feel affirmed in their own identities and see the powerful role they can play in fostering a more just and loving world. Supporting children's healthy racial identity development, and doing so through the use of intentional and explicit curriculum and pedagogy, should be recognized as foundational skills for early childhood teachers. Yet we have learned that, for a variety of reasons, many educators feel unprepared to do this work well. Additionally, we know that some teachers, in attempting to teach about these topics without having done the work they need to do to prepare for it, may do more harm than good. I hope that this book renews your commitment to growing in your capacity to do this work, fueled by the inspiration of the concrete examples of practices described by the educators who generously shared their stories. Additionally, these narratives might prompt the self-reflection and commitment to ongoing professional growth necessary to strengthen your own teaching practice.

Before we conclude, it is important to emphasize that teaching and learning about race and racism in early childhood education is not an isolated process but is situated in the web of intersectional, anti-bias curriculum and pedagogy (Derman-Sparks et al. 2020). The 2019 equity policy statement of the National Association for the Education of Young Children (NAEYC) reminds us that the ethics of our profession require us to work to resist bias and to dismantle systems of societal oppression that are mirrored in all of our systems and structures, including schools and early childhood programs. The statement specifies: "The biases we refer to here are based in race, class, culture, gender, sexual orientation, ability and disability, language, national origin, indigenous heritage, religion, and other identities" (4). The concept *intersectionality* was conceived by legal scholar Kimberlé Crenshaw when offering commentary on the Supreme Court confirmation hearings for Clarence Thomas. During the hearings, Thomas's former colleague Anita Hill testified about Thomas's pattern of sexual harassment. Crenshaw used the term *intersectional* to acknowledge that while Thomas experienced racial bias as a Black man, Hill's identity as a Black woman meant that she was subject to oppression along two dimensions of her identity. Understanding that we all hold intersectional identities reminds us to attend to the ways that we experience marginalization as well as privilege across a complex web of intersecting identity markers.

Each of us is shaped by intersectional identities, some of which subject us to bias and others that give us an unearned advantage. For instance, one aspect of a person's identity may make them part of a historically marginalized group subject to oppression or hate in the United States and elsewhere (such as being trans, or Muslim, or a speaker of a language other than English), while other aspects of that person's identity may result in receiving privilege and access to power that is not granted to others (such as being able-bodied, economically advantaged, or heterosexual). One aspect of our identity may feel more central to our sense of ourselves, but we are always experiencing the world (and being experienced by others) through the matrix of our complex and full intersectional identities. Anti-bias education (Derman-Sparks et al. 2020) demands that we work to confront all aspects of oppression and bias that are affected by our identities, and to partner with children and families in building a more just and loving future.

While our understanding of our own racial identity lives within our experience of our multifaceted intersectional identities, for the purposes of this book I have chosen to focus primarily on how we support young children's healthy racial identity development. This topic merits concerted attention for many reasons, not the least of which that the topics of race and racism are so difficult for many of us to speak about, especially for White educators. I have often witnessed White people like me shifting the focus away from our racial privilege when discussions of racism come up, choosing instead to highlight our own experiences of marginalization due to class status, religion, or gender identity. While many of us have experienced bias and oppression, it is important to give our undivided attention to strengthening our capacity to work against racial bias and prejudice. Before we can support young children's understanding of these issues, we must deepen our understanding of these issues for ourselves (Iruka et al. 2020; Rose 2024).

One example is the intersectional work of the educators organizing with the Black Lives Matter in Schools movement. The Black Lives Matter Movement emerged in response to the visibility of police killings of Black people. The early organizers of this movement were three Black queer women, Patrissa Cullors, Alicia Garza, and Opal Tometi. The principles of this movement have always been grounded in an intersectional stance that asserts that racial liberation that comes at the cost of reinforcing other forms of oppression is no liberation at all. As such, the principles of the Black Lives Matter in Schools movement insist that spaces for racial justice organizing must be queer and trans affirming, intergenerational, and free from sexism and misogyny. For an inspiring example of curriculum that illustrates these principles in ways that are culturally sustaining and developmentally appropriate for young children, early childhood teacher Laleña Garcia has produced two incredible resources that address these issues: *How We Can Live: Principles of Black Lives Matter* and *What We Believe: A Black Lives Matter Principles Activity Book*. Both books include engaging illustrations by Caryn Davidson and offer accessible prompts for teachers and short literacy activities and coloring book pages for young children to complete.

Additionally, this book is being written during a time when politicians and parents have amplified a moral panic about the perceived danger of talking about race and racism with young children. As this book is being prepared to go to press in 2025, many state and federal lawmakers are seeking to outlaw the right of schools and other institutions to intentionally address issues related to diversity, equity, and inclusion. These prohibitions prevent educators from doing the vital work of supporting children's healthy racial identity development by making it illegal to speak about race. In times like these, it is all the more important to document the powerful work that educators are doing to teach about race in ways that are affirming, culturally sustaining, and developmentally appropriate. It is my hope that parents, politicians, and educators who have concerns about talking about race and racism with young children can see ways to address these topics that offer healing rather than harm. There is an urgency to this work. We see so many instances of harm caused by fear of those who are different from us. We harm each other through institutional bias that grants some of us unearned power and privilege while justifying the marginalization and oppression of others. We cannot continue this way. By allowing ourselves to be divided, we miss opportunities for authentic connection. Our children want to join with us in building a more just and loving world. We owe it to them to make ourselves ready to do this uplifting, joyful, and powerful work.

References

Aladangady, Aditya, Andrew C. Chang, and Jacob Krimmel. 2023. "Greater Wealth, Greater Uncertainty: Changes in Racial Inequality in the Survey of Consumer Finances." FEDS Notes. Board of Governors of the Federal Reserve System, October 18. https://doi.org/10.17016/2380-7172.3405.

Alexander, Michelle. 2010. *The New Jim Crow: Mass Incarceration in the Age of Colorblindness.* The New Press.

Angier, Natalie. 2020. "Do Races Differ? Not Really, Genes Show." *New York Times,* August 22. www.nytimes.com/2000/08/22/science/do-races-differ-not-really-genes-show.html.

Barnes, Derrick. 2020. *I Am Every Good Thing.* Nancy Paulsen Books/Penguin.

Bifulco, Robert, and Sarah Souders. 2024. "Racial Disparities in School Poverty and Spending: Examining Allocations within Metropolitan Areas." *AERA Open* 10 (1).

Black Lives Matter at Schools, n.d. "Guiding Principles." Accessed July 11, 2025. www.blacklivesmatteratschool.com/guiding-principles.html.

Center for Anti-Racist Education. 2021. CARE Framework. https://integratedschools.org/wp-content/uploads/care_2021_framework_COMBO_v1.pdf.

Cherng, Hua-Yu Sebastian, and Peter F. Halpin. 2016. "The Importance of Minority Teachers: Student Perceptions of Minority versus White Teachers." *Educational Researcher* 45 (7): 407–20.

Cole, Kirsten. 2016. "Power Parents and the Gentrification of the PTA." In *Women Education Scholars and Their Children's Schooling,* edited by Kimberly A. Scott and Allison S. Henward. Routledge Research in Education. https://doi.org/10.4324/9781315736167.

Cole, Kirsten, and Diandra Verwayne. 2018. "Becoming Upended: Teaching and Learning about Race and Racism with Young Children and Their Families." *Young Children* 70 (2): 34–43. NAEYC. www.naeyc.org/resources/pubs/yc/may2018/teaching-learning-race-and-racism.

Cole, Kirsten, Jean-Yves Plaisir, Mindi Reich-Shapiro, and Antonio Freitas. 2019. "Building a Gender-Balanced Workforce: Supporting Male Teachers." *Young Children.* NAEYC.

Cooperative Children's Book Center. 2025. "CCBC's Diversity Statistics Show Promising Growth in Diverse Children's Books in 2024, but Room for Progress." March 13. https://uwmadison.app.box.com/s/rn4ccrdx8f8a2nbbqb6spx16kxcy52r1/file/1802253109720.

Crenshaw, Kimberlé. 1991. "Mapping the Margins: Intersectionality, Identity Politics, and Violence against Women of Color." *Stanford Law Review* 43 (6): 1241–99.

Delpit, Lisa. 2013. *Multiplication Is for White People: Raising Expectations for Other People's Children.* The New Press.

Derman-Sparks, Louise, Julie Olsen Edwards, and Catherine Goins. 2020. *Anti-Bias Education for Young Children & Ourselves,* 2nd ed. NAEYC.

Gao, Qin, Jianan Li, Ao Shen, and Xiaofang Liu. 2023. "Racial Discrimination Intensified while the Pandemic Subsided: Experiences of Chinese New Yorkers during 2020-2022." Columbia China Center for Social Policy. https://chinacenter.socialwork.columbia.edu/sites/chinacenter.socialwork.columbia.edu/files/content/News/Racial-Discrimination-Intensified-while-the-Pandemic-Subsided-2020-2022.pdf.

Garcia, Laleña. 2020. *What We Believe: A Black Lives Matter Principles Activity Book.* Lee & Low Books.

Garcia, Laleña. 2022. *How We Can Live: Principles of Black Lives Matter.* Lee & Low Books.

Garte, Rebecca, and Cara Kronen. 2020. "You've Met Your Match: Using Culturally Relevant Pairing to Cultivate Mentoring Relationships during the Early Practicum Experience of Community College Preservice Teachers." *Teacher Educator* 55 (4): 347–72.

Gasoi, Emily, and Deborah Meier. 2017. *These Schools Belong to You and Me: Why We Can't Afford to Abandon Our Public Schools.* Beacon Press.

Hannah-Jones, Nikole. 2016. "Choosing a School for My Daughter in a Segregated City." *New York Times,* June 9.

Harry, Beth, and Jeanette Klingner. 2022. *Why Are So Many Students of Color in Special Education?: Understanding Race and Disability in Schools,* 3rd ed. Teachers College Press.

Himley, Margaret, Lynne Strieb, Patricia Carini, Rhoda Kanevsky, and Betsy Wice, eds. 2002. *Prospect's Descriptive Processes: The Child, the Art of Teaching, and the Classroom and School.* The Prospect Center. https://digitalcollections.uvm.edu/view/35427/prospect-s-descriptive-processes-the-child-the-art-of-teaching-and-the-classroom-and-school.

Husband, Terry. 2012. "'I Don't See Color': Challenging Assumptions about Discussing Race with Young Children." *Early Childhood Education Journal* 39 (6): 365–71.

Iruka, Iheoma, Stephanie Currenton, Tonia Durden, and Kerry-Ann Escayg. 2020. *Don't Look Away: Embracing Anti-Bias Classrooms.* Gryphon House.

Jackson, Regina, and Saira Rao. 2022. *White Women: Everything You Already Know About Your Own Racism and How to Do Better.* Penguin Books.

Jones, Denisha. 2025. Fostering Healthy Identity Development in Young Children. Defending the Early Years. https://dey.org/fostering-healthy-identity-framework.

Katz, Karen. 2002. *The Colors of Us.* Square Fish.

Kendi, Ibram X. 2019. *How to Be an Antiracist.* One World.

Kissinger, Katie. 2014. *All the Colors We Are: The Story of How We Get Our Skin Color / Todos los colores de nuestra piel: la historia de por qué tenemos diferentes colores de piel.* Redleaf Press.

Ladson-Billings, Gloria. 1995. "Toward a Theory of Culturally Relevant Pedagogy." *American Educational Research Journal* 32 (3).

Lawrence-Lightfoot, Sarah. 2004. *The Essential Conversation: What Parents and Teachers Can Learn from Each Other.* Ballantine Books.

Lee, Stacey J. 2005. *Up Against Whiteness: Race, School, and Immigrant Youth.* Teachers College Press.

Lefkowits, Andrew. 2021. "Learning in Public with Courtney Martin." *Integrated Schools* podcast. August 4. https://integratedschools.org/podcast/martin.

Lester, Julius. 2008. *Let's Talk About Race.* HarperCollins.

Love, Bettina. 2019. *We Want to Do More than Survive: Abolitionist Teaching and the Pursuit of Educational Freedom.* Beacon Press.

Lutton, Linda, Andrew Fan, and Alden Loury. 2020. "Where Banks Don't Lend." WBEZ. https://interactive.wbez.org/2020/banking/disparity.

Madison, Megan, and Jessica Ralli. 2021. *Our Skin: A First Conversation About Race.* Rise x Penguin Workshop.

Martin, Courtney E. 2021. *Learning in Public: Lessons for a Racially Divided America from My Daughter's School.* Little, Brown and Company.

McGhee, Heather. 2021. *The Sum of Us: What Racism Costs Everyone and How We Can Prosper Together.* One World.

Menakem, Resmaa. 2017. *My Grandmother's Hands: Racialized Trauma and the Pathway to Mending Our Hearts and Bodies.* Central Recovery Press.

Moll, Luis C., Cathy Amanti, Deborah Neff, and Norma Gonzalez. 1992. "Funds of Knowledge for Teaching: Using a Qualitative Approach to Connect Homes and Classrooms." *Theory Into Practice* 31 (2): 132–41.

Morris, Monique. 2018. *Pushout: The Criminalization of Black Girls in Schools.* The New Press.

National Association for the Education of Young Children (NAEYC). 2019. "Advancing Equity in Early Childhood Education." Position statement. NAEYC. www.naeyc.org/resources/position-statements/equity.

National Center for Education Statistics. 2023b. "Characteristics of Public School Teachers." *Condition of Education.* US Department of Education, Institute of Education Sciences. https://nces.ed.gov/programs/coe/indicator/clr.

National Center for Education Statistics. 2023a. "Characteristics of Traditional Public, Public Charter, and Private School Teachers." *Condition of Education.* US Department of Education, Institute of Education Sciences. https://nces.ed.gov/programs/coe/indicator/sld.

National Center for Education Statistics. 2024. "Racial/Ethnic Enrollment in Public Schools." *Condition of Education.* US Department of Education, Institute of Education Sciences. https://nces.ed.gov/programs/coe/pdf/2024/cge_508c.pdf.

Noguera, Pedro A. 2003. "Schools, Prisons, and Social Implications of Punishment: Rethinking Disciplinary Practices." *Theory Into Practice* 42 (4): 341–50.

Noguera, Pedro A. 2012. "Saving Black and Latino Boys." *Phi Delta Kappan* 93 (5): 8–12.

Norwood, Kimberly Jade. 2015. "'If You Is White, You's Alright . . .' Stories About Colorism in America." *Washington University Global Studies Law Review* 14 (4): 585–607.

Oluo, Ijeoma. 2018. *So You Want To Talk About Race.* Hachette Book Group.

Paris, Django, and H. Samy Alim. 2017. *Culturally Sustaining Pedagogies: Teaching and Learning for Justice in a Changing World.* Teachers College Press.

Paschall, Katherine, Yuko Yadatsu Ekyalongo, and Christina M. Padilla. 2023. *Professional Characteristics of the Child Care and Early Education Workforce in 2012 and 2019: Descriptions by Race and Ethnicity, Languages Spoken, and Nativity Status.* OPRE Report #2023-205. Office of Planning, Research, and Evaluation, Administration for Children and Families (OPRE), US Department of Health and Human Services.

Rooks, Noliwe. 2025. *Integrated: How American Schools Failed Black Children.* Pantheon Books.

Rose, Courtney E. 2024. *Woven Together: How Unpacking Your Teacher Identity Creates a Stronger Learning Community.* John Wiley & Sons.

Schaeffer, Katherine. 2021. "America's Public School Teachers Are Far Less Racially and Ethnically Diverse Than Their Students." Pew Research

Center, December 10. www.pewresearch.org/short-reads/2021/12/10/americas-public-school-teachers-are-far-less-racially-and-ethnically-diverse-than-their-students.

Schaeffer, Katherine. 2024. "U.S. Public, Private and Charter Schools in 5 Charts." Rew Research Center, June 6. https://www.pewresearch.org/short-reads/2024/06/06/us-public-private-and-charter-schools-in-5-charts.

Sims Bishop, Rudine. 1990. "Mirrors, Windows, and Sliding Glass Doors." *Perspectives: Choosing and Using Books from the Classroom* 6 (3).

Stevenson, Bryan. 2014. *Just Mercy: A Story of Justice and Redemption.* Spiegel & Grau.

Sturdivant, Toni. 2023. *I Like Myself: Fostering Positive Racial Identity in Young Black Children.* Redleaf Press.

Sue, Derald Wing. 2003. *Overcoming Our Racism: The Journey to Liberation.* Jossey-Bass.

Tatum, Beverly Daniel. 1997. *Why Are All the Black Kids Sitting Together in the Cafeteria?: And Other Conversations About Race.* Basic Books.

Tervalon, Melanie, and Jann Murray-García. 1998. "Cultural Humility Versus Cultural Competence: A Critical Distinction in Defining Physician Training Outcomes in Multicultural Education." *Journal of Health Care for the Poor and Underserved* 9 (2): 117–25.

Turner, Cody, and Anya Kamenetz, hosts. 2019. *Life Kit: Parenting.* "Talking Race with Young Children." National Public Radio, April 26. Podcast.

United States Bureau of Labor Statistics. 2023. *Labor Force Statistics from the Current Population Survey.* www.bls.gov/cps/cpsaat11.htm.

Valdés, Guadalupe. 1996. *Con Respeto: Bridging the Distances Between Culturally Diverse Families and Schools: An Ethnographic Portrait.* Teachers College Press.

Walker, Alice. 1983. *In Search of Our Mothers' Gardens : Womanist Prose.* Harcourt Brace Jovanovich.

Will, Madeline. 2020. "Still Mostly White and Female: New Federal Data on the Teaching Profession." *Education Week,* April 14. www.edweek.org/leadership/still-mostly-white-and-female-new-federal-data-on-the-teaching-profession/2020/04.

Winkler, Erin. 2009. "Children Are Not Colorblind: How Young Children Learn Race." *PACE: Practical Approaches for Continuing Education* 3 (3): 1–8.

Index

All the Colors We Are: The Story of How We Get Our Skin Color (Kissinger), 28, 76
Angier, Natalie, 2
anti-racist teaching
    addressing concerns about, of families, 90–91
    effects on children of, ix
apple activity, 123
art, creating self-portraits, 27–28

Bank Street College of Education, 140
Barnes, Derrick, 78–79
Bishop, Rudine Sims, 25
Black Lives Matter in Schools movement, 149
Bridges, Ruby, 42

Carranza, Richard, 140
Center for Racial Justice in Education, 77
children
    absorption of racism by, 13, 36–37, 55
    benefits to, of having educators of global majority, 3–4
    curiosity as natural characteristic of, 1–2
    educators' learning expectations of, 101
    of global majority
        discipline in school of, 132–133
        racism experienced by, in educational settings, 114–117
        referrals to special education and, 110
        societal messages received by, 22
    importance of affirmation of identity of, 37
    messages about identity received by, 22
    as observers of actions of adults, 10–11
    racial identities of, in public schools in US, 3
    teaching, about race, 33–37
        All About Me units, 33–34
        with multiracial teams, 33–34
        using senses, 31–33
        when responding to children's observations and questions, 34–37
    teaching about racism
        fostering empathy and, 45–47
        foundation for, 63–64
        proactively before incidents, 61–62, 63–66
        when addressing incidents, 40–41, 48–54, 70–73, 114–117
    understanding of intersectional identities by, 21–22
White
    false sense of own superiority of, 16
    guilt and shame from learning about racism of, 10, 11, 90

resistance to teaching about racism by parents of, 112–114
societal messages received by, 22
children's literature, as presenting possibilities that might not yet exist in children's reality, 25–26
classroom libraries as "windows and mirrors," 25–26
colonialism, white supremacy as basis of, 6
color-evasiveness
  affirmation of identity and, 122
  defined, 4
  developments in racial reckoning and, 122
  effect of, on people of global majority, 59
colorism, internalization in communities of color of, 7–8, 59
The Colors of Us (Katz), 76–77
community
  knowing local, 83, 130
  restoring sense of, 41–42
Cooperative Children's Book Center (CCBC, University of Wisconsin-Madison), 25
Crenshaw, Kimberlé, 148
Critical Race Theory (CRT), 11
Cullors, Patrisse, 149
Curenton, Stephanie, 125
curiosity, as natural characteristic of children, 1–2
curriculum
  All About Me units, 33–34
  creating self-portraits, 27–28
  elements in designing, 13, 24
    cultures of backgrounds of children, 29–30, 97
    developmentally appropriateness of, 12–13
  Montessori, 29
  objections from families about, 90–91, 97–100
  Pollyanna, 82–83
  responsiveness to children of, 24
  support needed when developing, 68–69
  Teachers College Reading and Writing, 82
  using senses, 31–33
  See also resources

Davidson, Caryn, 149
Defending the Early Years, 4
Delpit, Lisa, 101
Diaz, Samantha R., ix–x
Don't Look Away: Embracing Anti-Bias Classrooms (Iruka, Curenton, Durden, and Escayg), 125
"Do Races Differ? Not Really, Genes Show" (Angier), 2
Durden, Tonia, 125

Early Head Start programs, 96, 140
education
  importance of culturally responsive, student-driven learning environment, 120
  importance of relevancy, 21
  types of racism in schools, 8–9
educators
  expectations of children, 101
  of global majority
    benefits to children of having, 3–4
    racism experienced by, 69–70
  identities of, as lens through which they teach, 14–15
  importance of addressing incidents of racism in schools, 114–117
  importance of culturally responsive mindset of, 120
  importance of development of, of all races, 30–31
  motivations for becoming, 127–129
  NAEYC on ethics of profession, 147–148

professional development experiences while teaching, 138–143, 145–146
racism in unexamined approach to teaching of, 123
referrals to special education by, 110
relationship between families and
  discomfort talking about race, 107–111
  educator's expectations of child and, 101
  openness to families' feedback, 98–100
  power dynamics and, 94
  racial/ethnic identities of each party and, 108–111
  sharing personal history to strengthen, 95
  talking about race, 102–105
  talking about racism, 105–107
  trust and, 39, 94
self-reflection on own identities by, 108, 120
teacher education of
  addressing unconscious biases that influence classroom discipline, 132–133
  affirmation of identity, 126
  alternative certification programs, 135
  community walks, 130
  coursework outside of teacher education credits, 135–136
  cultural bias based on white and Western expectations, 125
  development of cultural humility in, 125
  diverse ethnic and racial demographics of classmates and faculty, 136–138
  failure to address teaching about race and racism in, 124
  importance of diverse representation in materials used, 125
  internships, 129–130
  Montessori approach, 126
  preparation for building relationships with families, 130–132, 134–135
  resources for, 146
  role-play scenarios, 131
  self-reflection on biases and motivations for becoming educators, 127–129
  understanding of systemic racism, 133–134
  use of IAT, 126–127
  teams comprised of, of different races, 33–34
  White affinity groups, 143–144
equity, explaining, 84
Escayg, Kerry-Ann, 125
The Essential Conversation: What Parents and Teachers Can Learn from Each Other (Lawrence-Lightfoot), 111

families
  educators' discomfort talking to families about race, 107–111
  incorporation of cultural knowledge of, into curriculum, 97
  objections from, about curriculum, 90–91, 97–100
  objections of, to specific materials, 98
  philosophy of Early Head Start programs, 96
  reactions of, to teaching about racism, 66–67
  relationship between educators and
    educator's expectations of child and, 101
    power dynamics and, 94
    racial/ethnic identities of each party and, 108–111

receptiveness of educators to feedback from, 98–101
sharing of educator's personal history to strengthen, 95
talking about race, 102–105
talking about racism, 105–107
teacher education preparation for building, 130–132, 134–135
trust and, 39, 94
uncomfortableness in schools of, 95–96
First Conversations books (Madison and Ralli), 44
Freeman, Harold P., 2

Garcia, Laleña, 149
Garza, Alicia, 149
gender
discipline and, 132–133
referrals to special education and, 110
genetic makeup of humans, 2
girls, bodily autonomy of, 103–104
guilt, from learning about racism, 10, 11, 90

Hill, Anita, 148
holidays, 29–30
How We Can Live: Principles of Black Lives Matter (Garcia), 149

I Am Every Good Thing (Barnes), 78–79
identity/identities
affirmation of
child's, 23, 37, 104–105
race as aspect of, 122
in teacher education, 126
of educators
as lens through which they teach, 14–15
relationships with students' families and, 108–111
self-reflection on own, 108, 120
intersectional nature of, 21–22, 148

lifelong journey to fully understand own, 12
mapping with webs, 82
messages children receive about, 22
racial, of school-aged children in public schools in US, 3
racial, of teachers in US, 3
Implicit Association Test (IAT), 126–127
incarceration and institutional racism, 8
independent schools, 14
inequality "star" lesson, 45–46
Institutes on Descriptive Inquiry (IDI), 141
institutional racism, described, 8–9
Integrated Co-Teaching model, 87
internalized racism, described, 7–8
internships, 129–130
interpersonal racism, described, 8
intersectionality, 21–22, 148–149
Iruka, Iheoma, 125
"Is This Working?" (*This American Life* podcast), 132

Katz, Karen, 76–77
Kissinger, Katie, 28, 76

language, providing, for talking about race, 63–64
Lawrence-Lightfoot, Sarah, 111
learning
educators' expectations of children, 101
importance of culturally responsive, student-driven environment for, 120
through senses, 31–33
Lester, Julius, 83
Let's Talk About Race (Lester), 83
Life Kit: Parenting (podcast), 10–11
Love, Bettina, 144

Madison, Megan, 44, 77–78
Martin, Courtney, 60

materials
  designing own, 26
  families' objections to specific, 98
  importance of representation in, 125
  puppets, 73
  representations of people of all different races, 24–25
  using, as foundation for teaching about race and racism, 63
  See also resources
Menakem, Resmaa, 6
Montessori, Mari, 24
Montessori approach
  to curriculum, 29
  to teacher education, 126
Morris, Monique, 133
music, learning through, 32–33
My Grandmother's Hands: Racialized Trauma and the Pathway to Mending Our Hearts and Bodies (Menakem), 6

National Association for the Education of Young Children (NAEYC), 147–148
National Center for Education Statistics (US Department of Education), xiv, 3
National Public Radio, 10–11
New York Times, 2
N-word
  affectionate use of, xv
  racist use of, xiv, xv

Olson, Charles, xiii
Our Skin: A First Conversation About Race (Madison and Ralli), 44, 77–78

people of color. *See* people of global majority
people of global majority
  accuracy of term, 3
  as educators, 3–4, 69–70
  effect of color-evasiveness on, 59
  internalization of colorism by, 7–8, 59
  uncomfortableness in schools of, 95–96
Pew Research Center, 14
play, police–bad guy game, 67–68
podcasts, for learning about race and racism, 10–11, 18–19
police–bad guy play, 67–68
Pollyanna curriculum, 82–83
Powell, Tunette, 132
power dynamics, in relationship between families and educators, 94
private schools, 14
puppets, using, 73

race
  affirmation of, as aspect of identity, 122
  bodily autonomy and, 103–104
  changes in categories of, 6
  discipline and, 132–133
  educators' discomfort talking to families about, 107–111
  failure to acknowledge affirmation of identity and, 122
  defined, 4
  developments in racial reckoning and, 122
  effect of, on people of global majority, 59
  genetic makeup of humans and, 2
  importance of including nuances and complexities of, 144–145
  misconceptions about, 10
  purpose of myth of, 6
  relationship between educators and families and, 102–105, 108–111
  segregation and stereotypes, 75
  of teachers in US, xiv
  teaching about
    All About Me units, 33–34
    with multiracial teams, 33–34
    using senses, 31–33

when responding to children's observations and questions, 34–37
White parents' resistance to, 112–114
See also resources
wealth gap and, 58
xenophobic immigration laws, 7
racial colorblindness, 4, 59, 122
racial identity/identities
healthy development of, 23
of school-aged children in public schools in US, 3
of teachers in US, 3
racism
absorption by children of, 10, 13, 15, 36–37
compared to smog, 5, 122
in educators' unexamined approach to teaching, 123
experienced by educators of global majority, 69–70
guilt and shame caused by learning about, 10, 11, 90
importance of naming, 73
institutional, described, 8–9
internalized, described, 7–8
interpersonal, described, 8
relationship between educators and families and talking about, 105–107
stereotypes and, 123
teaching about
families' reactions to, 66–67, 112–114
fostering empathy and, 45–47
foundation for, 63–64
proactively before incidents, 61–62, 63–66
when addressing incidents, 40–41, 48–54, 70–73, 114–117
See also resources

as toxic combination of prejudice plus power, 7
unconscious biases and, 133
use of N-word, xiv, xv
Ralli, Jessica, 44, 77–78
resources
articles, 2
books, 5, 6, 25, 28, 44, 76–79, 83, 111, 120, 125, 144, 149
curriculums, 82–83
organizations, 25, 60, 77, 82, 140–141, 146
podcasts, 10–11, 18–19, 132
Responsive Classroom strategies, 40
restorative justice, described, 41–42
Rose, Courtney E., 120

segregation
de facto, 9
in housing, 10–11
racial stereotypes and, 75
self-portraits, 27–28, 76–77
senses, learning through, 31–33
Seuss, Dr., 44
shame, from learning about racism, 10, 11, 90
"skin-color recipe," 27–28
The Sneetches and Other Stories (Seuss), 44

"Talking Race With Young Children" (NPR podcast), 10–11
Tatum, Beverly Daniel, 5, 10–11, 122
Teachers College Reading and Writing curriculum, 82
This American Life? (podcast), 132
Thomas, Clarence, 148
Tometi, Opal, 149
trust and relationship between families and educators, 39, 94

Undoing Racism, 60

Verwayne, Diandra, 39

"warm demanders," 101
wealth gap and institutional racism, 8
We Want to Do More than Survive: Abolitionist Teaching and the Pursuit of Educational Freedom (Love), 144
What We Believe: A Black Lives Matter Principles Activity Book (Garcia), 149
White children
    false sense of own superiority of, 16
    guilt and shame from learning about racism of, 10, 11, 90
    resistance to teaching about racism by parents of, 112–114
    societal messages received by, 22
whiteness
    importance of naming, 77
    invisibility of, when dominant, 60
    physical attributes associated with, 8
    of teacher education of educators, 125
white supremacy
    colonialism and, 6
    internalization of harm caused by, 10, 13, 15, 36–37
    socialization into believing narrative of white superiority, 16
    willful ignorance of White people and, 17
Why Are All the Black Kids Sitting Together in the Cafeteria? And Other Conversations About Race (Tatum), 5
"windows and mirrors," 25
Woven Together: How Unpacking Your Teacher Identity Creates a Stronger Learning Community (Rose), 120

www.ingramcontent.com/pod-product-compliance
Lightning Source LLC
Chambersburg PA
CBHW081446070526
44586CB00019B/2244